HIDDEN HISTORY

of

Sarasota

HIDDEN HISTORY of Sarasota

JEFF LaHURD

THE
History
PRESS

Published by The History Press
Charleston, SC 29403
www.historypress.net

Copyright © 2009 by Jeff LaHurd
All rights reserved

First published 2009
Second printing 2012
Third printing 2013

ISBN 9781540219886

Library of Congress Cataloging-in-Publication Data

LaHurd, Jeff.
Hidden history of Sarasota / Jeff LaHurd.
p. cm.
Includes bibliographical references.
ISBN 9781540219886
1. Sarasota (Fla.)--History. 2. Sarasota (Fla.)--Social life and customs. I. Title.
F319.S35L328 2009
975.9'61--dc22
2009007731

This book is dedicated to my boyhood friend David P. Wernet, who was killed in Vietnam on August 18, 1967. The son of Mr. and Mrs. Paul A. Wernet, his Silver Star citation read, in part:

Although seriously wounded, Pfc. Wernet remained behind to place effective suppressive fire on the enemy and cover the platoon's withdrawal. When he began to withdraw, he was fatally wounded. Pfc. Wernet's outstanding valor and devotion to duty were in keeping with the highest traditions of the military service and reflect great credit upon himself, his unit, and the U.S. Army.

CONTENTS

FOREWORD

The Sarasota Alliance for Historic Preservation is pleased to sponsor, once again, Jeff LaHurd's latest book on our community's history, *Hidden History of Sarasota*. This book will look at Sarasota's development and colorful history from the time of the first settlers, through the land boom and real estate crash of the 1920s, the Great Depression of the 1930s, the post–World War II resurgence and the coming of Arvida at the end of the 1950s.

The Sarasota Alliance has claimed many successes since its inception in 1985. Among them are the restoration of Rosemary Cemetery, early restoration and relocations of the Crocker Church and the Bidwell-Wood House, relocation of the C.B. Wilson House, relocation of the Ringling Tack Room and our latest achievement, the relocation of a Siesta Key cottage and gentlemen's barn. These relocations were funded through the Alliance Revolving Fund, which continues to support preservation activities.

We host a well-acclaimed Historic Homes Tour annually and have joined in the publishing of many books on Sarasota's history. We are delighted to be part of Jeff LaHurd's newest venture.

Don Smally, President
Sarasota Alliance for Historic Preservation, Inc.
PO Box 1754
Sarasota, FL 34230

ACKNOWLEDGEMENTS

I would like to give a special thanks to the board of directors of the Sarasota Alliance for Historic Preservation for making this book possible. Without their support, *Hidden History of Sarasota* and many of the other books that I have written would not have been published.

Thank you to George I. "Pete" Esthus, a Sarasota historian in his own right, who has taken on the daunting task of being my "accuratizer." He proofed and made corrections for this book—no small feat. As always, I appreciate his effort.

I would like to thank Hope Black, Bertha Palmer biographer, for her assistance and for her dedication and hard work at the Sarasota County History Center.

I would also like to thank author Richard Wires for giving me the idea for this book.

I am finishing my fifth year as the Sarasota County history specialist at the Sarasota County History Center, and I would like to give a special thank-you to Lorrie Muldowney and Jodi Pracht for making coming to work each morning such a pleasure.

The History Center is located at 6062 Porter Way, and we invite you to come for research or to share your Sarasota photos and memorabilia with us and the community.

I would like to thank the Friends of the Sarasota County History Center for their support of the center during this difficult economic time.

Photographs in this book are from the Sarasota County History Center, the collection of George I. "Pete" Esthus, the John Hamilton Gillespie Collection, my personal collection and the Longboat Historical Society Collection.

THE EARLY YEARS

The landscape was so much more beautiful then than it is today. The thick virgin pine timber standing round and untouched. The tropical jungles and islands were greener, the water in the bays, bayous, creeks and rivers were bluer and clearer; the shore lines were straighter and cleaner; the beaches, both on the Gulf and inside waters were wider and much whiter…And the abundance of marine life, both fish and fowl, compared to what it is today is indescribable. The Indians had much more respect for what Mother Nature did for the humankind than the ruthless destructive hands of our present civilization
—Arthur Britton Edwards in an interview with Sarasota County historian Dottie Davis, July 23, 1958

NAMING SARASOTA

The origin of the name Sarasota has been the stuff of speculation for years. In the Mail Away edition of the *Sarasota Herald* from November 29, 1936, the following account is given:

> *Search the world over and you will find but one Sarasota. That Sarasota is in Florida on the state's beautiful west coast.*
>
> *Where did the name originate? Its residents have been trying to find out for years. The most logical explanation coming to this reporter's attention is one suggested by Mrs. Edna Mosely Landers.* [The reporter is not named.]
>
> *Old maps indicate the presence of a "Boca Sarazota." One such map was in the possession of the late Captain W.F. Purdy, dated 1776.*

According to the results of Mrs. Landers' investigation, Spanish explorers who passed this section of the west coast noted the presence of white sand Indian mounds which were on a level with the vegetation. From a distance, the whole looked flat and is said to have reminded the explorers of "Sahara."

What about the "sota" suffix?

The Indian word "zota" means clear, blue, limpid, beautiful. What more logical than that the "zota" was added to the Sahara and the two eventually became first "Sarazota" and then the present "Sarasota"? The "zota" probably was supplied by the Indians to Sarasota's beautiful bay which was in existence long before the Spaniards discovered this section. It has always charmed its beholders.

AGRICULTURE AND FISHING

In the long-ago days before Sarasota became a popular tourist haven, the local economy was dependent on cattle, farming and fishing.

William Whitaker brought the first herd of cattle to the area in 1847, and as more settlers came, thousands of acres were devoted to cattle ranching and the farming of various crops, particularly citrus, which thrived throughout what would become Sarasota County.

Early brochures that touted Sarasota advertised heavily the money-making opportunities inherent in the rich soil. As early as 1885, the Scots colonists were sold on the area by promises of the good life that awaited them as gentlemen farmers. While they were ill equipped to make a go of it in this hostile environment, many who followed them were quite successful.

As the 1896 *General Directory of Manatee County*, in which Sarasota was a small community, put it, "The groves of oranges, peaches, grape fruit and lemons are now proving a bonanza to the owners, while it has been demonstrated that fine tobacco can be grown near Sara Sota with great success." It was also noted that the "celery lands are practically inexhaustible."

Another selling point to attract would-be farmers was the ability to grow crops year-round—a real plus to a northern farmer who could not grow during the winter months.

Fruits and vegetables that could be grown and sold were many and varied, depending on the season. One proud farmer was quoted in the *General Directory of Manatee County* as telling a dinner guest:

The Early Years

Whatever you see before you, good or bad, was grown on my farm right here—the meats, the bread, the turkey, the chicken, the sugar, the syrup, the potatoes and vegetables of all kinds before you, were grown on my place.

The following were listed in the Manatee directory as bountiful crops to grow and sell:

Oranges ten months in the year; plums, peaches, pears and grapes in the summer; hay, corn, potatoes, Bermuda onions and other products come in the fall. Then, cotton, cane, tobacco and all field crops still further diversify the farmers' products and increase the farms' prosperity.

Reports of the various crops that were harvested and sold to northern markets, the number of boxes or carloads and the amount of money they fetched were printed daily in the *Sarasota Times* newspaper.

Cattle ranchers had thousands of acres on which their herds could graze and fatten for sale. During the summer months, when a beef cow was butchered, a piece of the animal would be sold to each of the nearby families so that it could be immediately cooked and not spoil.

Fishing in Sarasota waters—the gulf, bay, rivers and creeks—was unsurpassed anywhere, and it was not only a good food source for the locals but was also the first attraction for early tourists. Sure to be included in literature touting Sarasota's virtues were stories of huge catches of tarpon, kingfish, mackerel, mullet, pompano, trout, redfish and snook. Also bountiful were oysters, clams, scallops and crabs. The day's catches were often strung up at hotels and boardinghouses for photo ops and bragging rights.

It was reported in 1919 that one man caught 12,570 pounds of fish in twenty-two days, and A.B. Edwards recalled that a school of fish entered the bay in the morning, kept moving northward all day long and was still in sight when darkness fell. He was quoted in Karl Grismer's *The Story of Sarasota*: "The fish were so thick you would hit them with your oars, and into the boat they'd plop."

EARLY HEALTHCARE

For the most part, settlers in the Sarasota area had to self-treat the wounds, infections and illnesses that befell them. Dr. Furman Chairs Whitaker, son of William and Mary Whitaker, opened his practice here in 1896 but moved to Manatee a year later. In 1904, Dr. Jack Halton opened his practice, and in 1908 he opened the Halton Sanitarium.

According to the late Adam Westcott, former research assistant volunteer at the Sarasota County History Center from whom most of this information is derived, the mother was the healer in the family:

Each family kept a kitchen garden near the house, which included commonly used medicinal herbs such as dried palmetto berries or pennyroyal tea for colds and flu; soda and ginger for colic; honey, lemon juice or horehound for coughs; cinnamon or nutmeg for diarrhea; willow bark tea for fever; oak bark tea or a drop of turpentine on a lump of sugar for worms; chewed tobacco poultice for insect stings; and kerosene or animal fat for wounds.

Colds were often dealt with by using a mustard plaster on the chest, wrapping the patient in a blanket and resting for at least 24 hours. Indeed, the warm climate itself was recommended by northern doctors for many diseases such as consumption (tuberculosis).

The pioneer housewife did have access to several home health medical books for guidance, as well as advice from other women in the area. Patients with more difficult or persistent cases might be treated by a more experienced "herb woman" or taken to a doctor. Babies were usually delivered at home by a midwife, family members or neighboring women.

The 19th century doctor was not a quack, practicing medicine willy-nilly without a theory. Most doctors subscribed to the Brunonian theory of disease which stated that disease was caused by excessive "excitement" in the body. The idea of treatment was to reduce the "excitement." Malaria, often called Intermittent Fever and a scourge of our semi-tropical environment was thought to be caused by breathing air contaminated by rotting vegetation in swampy areas.

Doctors believed that some people were "disposed" to certain diseases, while others could be exposed to the same disease and not be affected. The germ theory of disease did not become the basis of treatment until the late 19th century, and antibiotics did not appear until the 1930s.

Other treatment options included purging the stomach, purging the bowel, bleeding and the use of leeches. For the hardy pioneers who braved this wilderness, illness was just another of life's burdens that they had to endure.

THE SETTLEMENT ACT OF 1842

The Settlement Act of 1842 provided 160 acres of land to those who would homestead here for five years and, if necessary, take up arms against the Seminole Indians, whom the federal government was trying to remove from Florida.

SURVEYING THE WILDERNESS

On a bright spring day in 1885, Sarasota pioneer Arthur B. Edwards and his father were out hunting when they came upon a group of strangers surveying the wilderness. The men, hired by the Florida Mortgage and Investment Company, a Scottish concern, had hacked out a ten-foot area and were drawing a bead on a red-and-white pole stuck in the ground at the bay's high-water mark, today's Gulf Stream Avenue. The imaginary line to the pole would become lower Main Street, and the spot on which they stood is today the center of Five Points. While father and son silently watched, the engineer, Richard Paulson, announced grandly, "We will lay out the town of Sarasota from this hub."

DEPARTING SCOTLAND

In recalling the departure of the Scots colony settlers from their homeland, Nellie Lawrie, a child at the time, remembered:

> It was a terrible, dark and rainy night when the people left Scotland. A large crowd gathered to see them start for America. As they gathered together on Groenock [Greenock?] Pier, waiting for the tender to take them out to the Furnesia, many felt very sad and worried. Such a long journey in those days to a new country was quite an undertaking.
>
> Someone in the crowd feeling that emotion was getting too much for the people started that old Scottish song: "Will ye not come back again? Better loved ye ne'er will be."
>
> As the tender slowly pulled away, the colonists and the people on the pier started to sing together as they never sang before: "Should auld acquaintance be forgot and never brought to mind." Few of the crowd

Lewis Colson, Sarasota's first black settler, and his wife, Irene. Lewis came to assist the engineer of the Florida Mortgage and Investment Company in 1884. The Colsons helped to organize the Bethlehem Baptist Church, Sarasota's first black church, and were very active in the black community. *Courtesy of the Sarasota County History Center.*

could sing the first verse, "We'll meet again soon ither night, for the days of Auld Lang Syne," for there were tears in their eyes and a sob in their throats.

The last song heard from the colonists as the captain gave the signal to start for America, was that beloved old hymn: "My Faith Looks Up to Thee."

Pity the poor Scots. They sold their worldly possessions, took what they could easily transport and set sail for America. After a rough, transatlantic crossing to New York, it was down to Fernandina, Florida, through Gainesville and Cedar Key, and finally, on a cold December morning in 1885, they pulled into beautiful Sarasota Bay, near where Marina Jack is today.

Even from the ship's rail they could tell that they had been duped; "Little Scotland" was a wilderness with which they were unprepared to deal.

Moffat, Scotland, the hometown of Gillespie. It was from such towns and villages as this that the Scots colony came. They were not equipped to deal with the rugged wilderness they found Sarasota to be. *John Hamilton Collection. Courtesy of the Sarasota County History Center.*

Alex Browning, who was a boy at the time, wrote of the experience in his memoirs in 1932. His story picks up as his boat, the *Governor Safford*, sailed toward Sarasota Bay:

> *We passed the day somehow, sailing along past Egmont Lighthouse, and on to Sarasota Pass then into Sarasota Bay where a landing was made at a small temporary wharf, evidently built to be used by fish boats.*
>
> *It was late in the afternoon when we landed at last, arriving at our destination, SARASOTA, where we were met by the other colonists and Mr. Tate who had come ahead of us on the lumber schooner from Cedar Key as well as all the natives for miles around who had expected us for some time. Amongst them was the Whitaker family, Riggins, Abbeys, Tuckers, Tatums, and T.M. Weir who had charge of the company store at the foot of [the] wharf. Mr. A.C. Acton was manager for the company at this time, he being like ourselves, lately arrived from the old country, did not know how to handle a colony of this size and Tate had lost the confidence of us by this time, the result was confusion all around.*
>
> *Of course there was much discontent, being dumped like this, in a wild country without houses to live in; tired and hungry, one can imagine what it was like. Families grouped around their mothers, while their fathers were trying to find out where they were going to live. The Company store being the only building in sight, the dirt road being faintly seen, leading through the pine and palmetto scrub.*

RAIN, RAIN AND RAIN

Anton Kleinoscheg preceded the Scots colony to Sarasota, arriving here earlier in 1885. Writing to a friend on July 28, 1886, he related:

> *And now to me. We are at the peak of the rainy season; rain, rain, and rain, If it rained on schedule a few hours each day, I should not object to this phenomenon; but one week ago we had rain keeping on for 36 hours, and today a repetition of this spectacle seems to take place. Under such circumstances I can't work and the enormous quantities of water streaming into my low clearing destroy or damage the small achievements that have been completed so far. Sometimes I think of my Cary (oh yes, you don't know that I am in love and the aspirant for marriage; well, we will return to this point…)*

Anton Kleinoscheg on his front porch. An early settler to Sarasota, he had a rough go of it here. He described the mosquitoes as "beasts" and said they were so bad that they killed two of his dogs. *Courtesy of the Sarasota County History Center.*

The climate in winter (though we had a cold never experienced before last winter) is very pleasant and wholesome; but the summer!—100 degrees F. when it is not raining, and the terrible plague of the mosquitoes. Enough to drive us mad! Well, "you don't walk unpunished under palm trees" says, I think, some great Nicco poet; and the painting with petroleum, in which condition I must necessarily write these lines (the only manner), is less than pleasant. You can imagine that I look with rather unfriendly eyes at the clouded sky which constantly sends down the water masses that stand in ponds and depressions and generate millions of these beasts. They have in fact killed two of my young dogs (a horrible end).

I sleep under a bar of course, otherwise sleep would be impossible, but in the miserable hut in which I am living (it belongs to the Abbes) no screen; therefore, it is impossible to burn a light; I go to bed at half past seven as soon as it grows dark, then I light the lamp and read behind the bar. But on the clearing at work I fall a victim to their bloodthirstiness, and I think no girl can await her sweetheart with so much longing as I am awaiting the end of the rainy season—still two months. Only then will I be a man.

Kleinoscheg married Carrie Abbe, who, with her mother Charlotte, had nursed him back to health when he fell ill with malaria. Carrie was the daughter of Charles E. Abbe, the postmaster who was assassinated by the Sarasota Vigilantes in 1884.

Later the couple moved to Staatz in Austria, where, according to a descendant, Anton Kleinoscheg Whitaker, in the self-published *One Man's Family (in Seven Parts)*, he found employment. But his health worsened, and "after a period of intense suffering," he died in 1900 and is buried in Central Cemetery, Vienna, Austria.

The couple had one child, Cecile. In September 1900, Carrie and Cecile moved back to America, to live with her mother in Elgin, Illinois. Cecile married in 1920 and died in childbirth in 1923, as did her baby.

ALONE IN THE WOODS

The struggles endured by the colonists were also noted in the diary of Dan McKinlay, excerpted in the *Sarasota Sunday Tribune* in October 1937. Obviously frustrated and disheartened by his surroundings, this gentleman from Scotland who had come in search of a new life wrote of the nightmares he and the others faced:

> *Dec. 29—Picture us alone in the woods in our little log hut. It's a queer experience, and I can't describe it. I am going to light my pipe for I feel very sad.*

The situation for the group unraveled quickly:

> *Jan. 11, 1886—The night was awfully cold. We kept a large fire on the hut all night but could not keep out the cold...morning temperature nine degrees below freezing point and today snow fell for the first time in 30 years...I am startled by a man riding up to the hut door. His name is Riggins...sent up to examine our land, it having been hinted to him by someone that it is under laid with hardpan...In an hour's time he came back with Tom and alas, our worst fears are realized. Our land is useless.*
>
> *Jan. 21—Started off to find Brown's place...I try to find the proper trail, but must have taken the wrong one...the more I search the more confused I get...Tramping through thick undergrowth, now through high palmetto, my thoughts rigidly fixed on the formidable rattlesnake...Through*

saw grass higher than my self, at last arrive at Whitakers ford on Phillipe creek...After two hours walk I arrive at log hut and am pleased to find it is the place I am in search of.

Jan. 26—The colony is breaking up very fast...Mr. Galloway, Beerton and Watson being away looking at another place in orange country.

Jan. 27—It is really very lonely...the eerie sound of the owl...the night is pitch dark...queer sounds...am going to turn in...have big washing to do in the morning.

Feb. 1—Thinking seriously of going to Jacksonville...no church here... weary to get to one.

Feb. 2—Prairie on fire all around us...grand sight...fires miles in extent burning up everything in their way.

Feb. 4—Prospects here are so bad...in fact as far as we can see it means starvation if we stay...again see prairie fires some distance from us...high wind blowing and some rain...the colony seems to have completely broken up.

Feb. 7—Growing more and more of opinion that we can't make a living here. Evening—prairie again on fire and close to us...creeps close upon us...almost as soon as it is done the wind shifts and threatens to burn us out.

Able to take it no longer, the March 11 entry reads: "About noon we hear the whistle and get on board...All Sarasota is turned out to see us off."

The plight of the Scot colony was expressed by A.B. Edwards in an interview with the *Sarasota Herald* in 1935: "Their distress and humiliation and the hardships they encountered can scarcely be expressed in words."

JOHN HAMILTON GILLESPIE

In 1874, John Hamilton Gillespie received a letter from Professor of Astrology L. Thomson of Kansas City, Missouri, which informed him of some bad news:

Your planetary aspects for the coming year are not favorable. It is indicated that about the first of February you will enter into a speculation that will prove unfortunate. It is also indicated that you will hear news of other unfavorable investments in which you are interested, during the summer. You

John Hamilton Gillespie stands next to his carriage with his manservant, Leonard Reid, who is about to drive Gillespie's fiancée, Blanche, into town. *Courtesy of the Sarasota County History Center.*

will receive letters of considerable importance to you in the next two months, and they will cause you to make some change in your plans. You will have a pleasant year, socially. You will get along well with your associates and will not have enemies. The people with whom you deal will be quite honorable in their treatment of you.

Venus indicates that there will not be true congeniality between yourself and companion. It is indicated that in the next year you will take some steps toward a legal separation.

Mercury is moderately favorable to your health, though you are threatened with a slight illness in the spring. You are not in danger of serious accidents.

(Dictated). L Thomson

Gillespie must have had faith in L. Thomson. He received correspondence from him from the 1850s through 1906.

Alex Browning, a young man when he arrived in Sarasota with his parents, said of Gillespie:

John Hamilton Gillespie practices his swing. He loved his golf. *Courtesy of the Sarasota County History Center.*

Colonel Gillespie often played with his friends and frequently invited them to join him in a golf match. He was a big-framed, jovial fellow and the natives and early settlers soon came to look upon him as a great big boy who could take a joke and was always ready to do a good turn for his neighbors.

THE KILLING OF POSTMASTER ABBE

The killing of Postmaster Abbe in 1884 was reported throughout the nation, including a story in the *New York Times* headlined "An Assassination Society: The Bloody Work of a Band of Southern Murderers." The article went on to tell the tale of the killing by, among others, Alfred Bidwell, "a former citizen of Buffalo, in good repute, who now lives in Sarasota, Fla." The killing had been planned at his house.

According to historian Vernon E. Peeples in *The Sarasota Democratic Vigilantes,* the group was formed in 1884 for the purpose of "mutual protection and the punishment of those whom the law could not reach, or, in other words, the removal of all obnoxious persons."

Abbe, who was seen as aiding land-grabbers in a scheme to take over some homesteads, was shotgunned, his throat was cut and then his body was loaded onto a boat and taken to the Gulf of Mexico, where it was thrown to the sharks. It was never recovered.

Ultimately the killers were rounded up by a posse from Manatee, and at the beginning of May 1885, the first of three trials was held at the county seat at Pine Level. Prison sentences were meted out; some of the men escaped and three were sentenced to hang but never did.

The incident spelled the end of the Sarasota Vigilantes, who were called "a notorious Sarasota assassination society."

Longtime resident Fannie Crocker Curtis justified the murder. In a 1958 interview with Sarasota County historian Dottie Davis, when told that the killers were a bunch of cutthroats, Curtis responded:

> *No, they weren't no bunch of cutthroats. They were good men, every one of them were good men. There weren't any cutthroats about it, and the person who told you that just told you something that wasn't so! You take Joe Anderson, Louis Cato, J. Alford, all those people I knew. You couldn't have found better men; they were fighting for their rights! They didn't want those people coming in here and killing their stuff up like they were doing it, and not using it at all. They were buying up all the orange groves they could…and Andrews was a doctor. And old man Bidwell was a* [not clear] *he had a store down there at the end of* [not clear]. *They were big men and they wanted to try to rule everything. They made trouble.*

ROSE WILSON

When Rose Wilson arrived here with her husband, Cornelius Van Santvoord Wilson, in 1899, Sarasota was still a rugged, one-horse town of two hundred souls, with little to commend save its exquisite virginal beauty and tropical climate.

We were but a small part of Manatee County in those pioneer days, no different from the other settlements that dotted the area: Manatee, Terra Ceia, Braidentown, Miakka and a dozen more.

Rose Wilson took over the publication of the *Sarasota Times* upon the death of her husband, C.V.S. Wilson, in 1910 and never missed an issue. With her is Brownie. *Courtesy of the Sarasota County History Center.*

There was a post office here, a few mercantile businesses, the De Soto Hotel and the Sarasota boardinghouse, for "those visitors who have to practice economy." We also had a livery and blacksmith shop, and people mostly made their livings working the land, raising cattle, farming, fishing and hunting.

Train service had not started yet, and our connection to the outside world was by way of the steamer *Mistletoe*, which came from Tampa on Monday, Wednesday and Friday to deliver supplies.

In spite of the odds, Cornelius was determined to establish a newspaper here, and with Rose's support and assistance, he began publishing the *Sarasota Times* in a small wooden building on lower Main Street.

After Cornelius died in 1910, Rose took over the operation of the paper and became its reporter, editor and publisher. She never missed an issue.

A progressive woman who saw Sarasota's potential as a resort haven, Rose editorialized strongly for the break away from Manatee County so that Sarasota could move forward, pushed for educational opportunities for

Looking toward the dock, 1909. In 1911, Dr. William E., J.O. and Frank B. Hover, who wintered here from Lima, Ohio, purchased the dock from Harry Higel. In 1913, they built what became known as the Hover Arcade, for many years the site of city hall. The building to the left is Badger's Drugs. Note the trough in the center of Five Points. *Courtesy of the Sarasota County History Center.*

Sarasota's children, supported the right of women to vote and lobbied for the construction of the Tamiami Trail, a road that linked Tampa with Miami.

In 1923, with the paper an established success and Sarasota about to be transformed by the real estate boom, Rose sold, noting in her last editorial, "Now that larger plans speak of a greater Sarasota there are none who feel a greater interest and pride than those, who in the pioneer days caught the vision and paved the way."

Rose, who died in 1964, was one of the first of many Sarasota women who, individually and in groups, caught the vision and helped pave the way to Sarasota's success as a vibrant county. How proud she must have felt for her role in its success!

LIFE IN THE PIONEER DAYS

In discussing how settlers made a living during the pioneer days in Sarasota, Arthur Britton Edwards, who was born here in 1874 and was a major player in the community's success, related to county historian Dottie Davis in a 1959 interview that settlers survived

> *mainly off the natural resources of the land and water. The hollow trees were full of honey; the woods full of game; the waters teaming with all kinds of fish. The jungles and the wild forests were full of all kinds of wild berries such as huckleberries, grapes and the like; cattle, hogs and sheep roamed the free range; fertile soil for the farmers, wild citrus and tropical fruit aplenty. In the woods were plenty of game, animals and fowl in abundance. No canning or processing in those early days; everything was fresh off the hoof, off the vine, off the tree, cut out of the soil or out of the water or wrapped in hide or feathers. Therefore the pioneer's main concern was his shot gun and shot bag, his rifle, his gun caps, his buck shot and powder, a dry powder horn, a waterproof match box, his blowing horn, a sharp knife and his dog.*

Edwards, along with J.H. Lord, was responsible for attracting Mrs. Palmer to the area from Chicago and selling her vast tracts of land. He was also instrumental in establishing Myakka River State Park and was the first mayor of the city of Sarasota. His accomplishments were so many and varied for this area, which he loved so much, that he was known as Mr. Sarasota. He died on November 14, 1969, having seen the wilderness in which he was born blossom into a beautiful county.

GILLESPIE AND BRIGHT EYES

The following is a letter from John Hamilton Gillespie to his fiancée, Blanche McDaniel, written when she was in Washington, D.C., and about to come to Sarasota for their wedding:

Sarasota, Florida. 12th April 1905

My Darling Little One:

This is not my regular letter to you, but I see from your tone of your letters that you have little hope of getting started before next Monday, and as you did me the great compliment of asking to see my Easter essay, I have this morning cut and carved it, and send it herewith for your approval. Darling, I want to know what you really think of it, as I am anxious to make a creditable appearance. I know you will tell me true.

The last two pictures are scenes from places where I trust you will be with me in June. Then you can understand the writing better. Don't forget to bring it back with you, and on our way home, you can lecture me on the subject. Bright Eyes I cannot write nice Love Letters in an office on a type writer, and this does not count as a Letter. Your Victrola has come, and your father is down looking at it. It will be ready for my dear Little Queen when she returns. Lots of people interrupt me, so Prettiest of Pretty "Yankees" with fond kisses, adieu, until I write you tonight on my return from W.W.R. Now Please do not think me conceited in sending you my essay, but I really want you to give me your opinion.

Ever Your Loving
Hamilton Gillespie

Blanche first came to Sarasota to visit her parents in 1902 and described what it was like arriving in what was basically a frontier town:

I traveled by train to Sarasota, a town I had never seen. It was a frightening experience for a young girl coming to her new home for the first time and stepping off the train into a complete black void. Under the weight of my bag I felt my feet sink into the sand. There was not a human being around and the only thing I could see was a dim oil lamp burning in the station master's office. My mother and father were not there to meet me, as the train had arrived twenty minutes ahead of schedule. The conductor told me to wait in the office until the train was turned around and put away for the night. He came and took me by my hand and pulled me through the darkness and sand halfway down Main Street from the Seaboard Railway station on Lemon Avenue towards the waterfront. At last I met my mother and father who were on their way to meet me. I was never so glad in my life to see them as I was at that moment.

Gillespie and Blanche were married in Sarasota on May 23, 1905, at the Episcopal church. The *Sarasota Times* called it the "Prettiest Wedding

John Hamilton Gillespie's second wife, Blanche McDaniel, at the time of their wedding. He called her "my darling little Bright Eyes." Blanche outlived John by twenty-five years. She died at the home of her sister in Doylestown, Pennsylvania, on December 31, 1958. *Courtesy of the Sarasota County History Center.*

in Sarasota," tagging Gillespie as "the Golfing Mayor" and Blanche "the charming and accomplished daughter of Judge and Mrs. R.P. McDaniel."

The paper reported that their romance had begun on the Sarasota Golf Links, which Gillespie had laid out, and offered, "Kindhearted, genial loyal to his friends and a gentleman to the manor born, Col. Gillespie is universally liked and he is most to be congratulated for the sweet and loving companion he has won."

After a celebratory breakfast at their future home, Rosebourne, the couple was driven to the Seaboard train depot, "where they boarded a private car and were whirled away amidst a shower of rice, old shoes, golf sticks and good wishes."

They would honeymoon in Washington and then go on to New York, where they would take the Anchor Line steamship *Caledonia* for Scotland, Gillespie's birthplace.

The home of John Hamilton Gillespie on Links Avenue. Later this would be the site of the Robarts Funeral Home. *Courtesy of the Sarasota County History Center.*

FRUITFUL ADVERTISING

On January 23, 1910, in the Real Estate/Farm Lands section of the *Chicago Sunday Tribune*, there appeared an advertisement that would change, or at least speed up, the course of the history of Sarasota County:

> *FLORIDA. Grapefruit and Orange Groves. Beautiful Winter Homes. Fruit and Vegetable Lands in the famous Sarasota Bay district of Manatee County on the gulf. I am one of the largest growers and land owners in Manatee County and can furnish you with any kind or size property desired. I also improve lands and raise groves for purchasers. Best location in U.S. Lowest prices. Easy terms. Call or write for free book and full information. J.H. Lord, owner, 922 Marquette Bldg.*

Mrs. Potter Palmer read the ad and decided to come with her family for a look-see. Their arrival by train was reported in the *Sarasota Times* on February 24.

The Early Years

They were to have been lodged in the Belle Haven Inn Hotel (formerly the De Soto) but instead were given rooms in the Halton Sanitarium, which was felt to have been in better condition to care for such august company.

News of the arrival was not banner headline material in the *Sarasota Times*, which devoted most of its front page to advertisements and a comprehensive article, "Saving Florida Lands."

But on the bottom of page three, in the fourth column, it was reported:

Arrival of Mrs. Potter Palmer. The most distinguished party recently visiting Sarasota, consisting of Mrs. Potter Palmer, her son, Honore Palmer, her father, Judge Honore, H.H. Honore and A.C. Honore, all of Chicago. They had telegraphed from Chicago for four rooms with baths at the Belle Haven Inn, but the rooms with baths being all occupied at that hotel, Mr. Whipple the proprietor engaged apartments for them at the Halton, where they will remain for some time.

Mrs. Palmer is one of the widest known American women and is almost as well known in London and Paris as in her home city Chicago. She is a beautiful woman and her portrait often appears in periodicals as an example of American beauty. Mrs. Palmer sails in a few days for London, where she will entertain during the social season at their London residence on Carlton House Terrace.

Dr. Jack Halton took Mrs. Palmer and party out fishing Wednesday and they caught several fish in the Pass.

Mrs. Palmer is so well pleased with Sarasota and vicinity that she will extend her visit several days beyond the time originally anticipated.

To Col. J.H. Lord is due the credit of inducing this distinguished party to make this visit.

Mrs. Palmer would soon buy thousands of acres of property in the area, and her pronouncements about Sarasota's beauty were reported in the major newspapers, piquing the interests of others who would follow her down, particularly from Chicago and the Northeast.

Sarasota was on its way to realizing its town motto: "To Grow and Prosper."

The all-brick, fire-proof Tonnelier Building on the south side of lower Main Street housed the Palms Hotel, Dr. Joe Halton's office, a café and a theatre. It burned to the ground in 1915. The city was awaiting delivery of its new fire truck. *Courtesy of the Sarasota County History Center.*

REAL ESTATE

A very important real estate transaction was noted on the inside page of the May 26, 1910 *Sarasota Times*. Mr. Owen Burns, described as a wealthy banker from Chicago who was staying at the Halton Hotel (formerly the Halton Sanitarium) on Gulf Stream Avenue, purchased the holdings of John Hamilton Gillespie, including the Gillespie home, bank building, golf grounds and other valuable property such as the Halton, which he would transform into his family home. The purchase price was $35,000, and Burns became the owner of what would be 75 percent of today's city limits. He would go on to be Sarasota's first major developer and a key player in Sarasota's 1920s success billing itself as a desirable destination for wealthy snowbirds.

For his part, John Hamilton Gillespie, who had been sent to Sarasota by the Florida Mortgage and Investment Company to revive the failed Scots colony in 1886, planned to sail to Scotland for a much-needed rest. The gentleman who had been the first mayor of the town of Sarasota and laid out the first golf course in Florida, and one of the first in the nation, would

Built by Gillespie in 1905, this building at Main Street and Pineapple Avenue housed Sarasota's first library and first bank, as well as a number of businesses. Most notably, it was Badger's Drug Store for many years. The building was razed in 1964. *Courtesy of the Sarasota County History Center.*

return and remain active in the civic affairs of the city. He suffered a heart attack while walking what had been his beloved golf course and died on September 7, 1923.

Death by Whiskey

On October 26, 1911, Mr. Charles E. Hall of Tampa died. He was found sitting at a table in a room on the Higel Dock (near today's Marina Jack). According to the newspaper headline, "Death by Whiskey" was the cause of Mr. Hall's untimely demise.

He and two friends had been playing cards throughout the evening and drinking as they played. Hall, over the protestations of the others, poured himself an especially large glass of demon whiskey, downed it and put his head on the table. The others thought he was sleeping. One left and the other went to bed. An inquest was held and determined: "We the jury find that Chas. E. Hall, deceased, came to his death while drinking an overdose of whiskey while in a physically weak condition."

It was determined that the whiskey had been sold by Jason Burke, who was held for trial. However, someone furnished Jason with a hacksaw, and he cut his way out of jail and escaped.

The decedent, who had worked for the Sarasota Cigar Company, was thirty-nine years old.

LIPS THAT TOUCH TOBACCO

Back in the day when a manly man could take a whiff off of a cheroot, blow out a puff of smoke and pronounce, "A woman is only a woman, but a good cigar is a smoke" and not get slapped across his pie hole, Sarasota had a cigar manufacturing business.

It was nothing to match Tampa's burgeoning Ybor City to be sure, but the Sarasota Cigar Company was a welcome addition to a community then struggling to bolster its economy.

In 1911, when John H. Hill and his family started the enterprise, Sarasota looked very much like the back lot of the western *Shane*—which is to say, there was very little here to distinguish it from a number of other cow towns.

Inasmuch as a cigar factory could be a benefit to the fledgling community, Mr. Hill approached the board of trade to get it to ante up some money to assist in the building of a factory. Up to that point, the Hill family had been rolling cigars in their home on Main Street.

Ten dollars was promptly pledged by Dr. Schultz, the proprietor of Badger's Drug Store. At the same meeting, businessman John Savarese grandly prophesized that in the near future a workforce of some two hundred men was possible. How much of a difference those ten dollars made is not known, but Hill was evidently happy to get it and the vote of confidence that went with it. At the next meeting, he demonstrated his appreciation by presenting the board with a box of cigars, with the pearl that "they were a hit with railroad people." Who better to judge a good smoke?

Initially, the company offered three brands: Board of Trade (amazing how much goodwill ten dollars bought!), Sarasota and the Sarasota Gem. Soon, Little Dixie, Simpatica and Habana were added to the line.

A COOL SMOKE

AS YOU LIKE IT
without the aid of a cake of ice or a fan. A fine cool smoke can be obtained every time you smoke a
LITTLE DIXIE CIGAR
They are hand made and have all the qualities that appeal to the critical smoker. The price is only 5 cents.

Sarasota Cigar Com.

A cigar advertisement for the Sarasota Cigar Company—filling Sarasota's, if not the country's, need for "a good five cent cigar." Courtesy of the Sarasota County History Center.

After a month's production, nearly ten thousand stogies had been rolled and sold through local businesses and also in Bradentown and faraway Tampa. Even during the summer, business was said to be "very satisfactory."

The *Sarasota Times* soon reported that the factory (still in Hill's Main Street home) employed four workers and that output had doubled every month since the enterprise began.

Hill took on the role of traveling salesman, drumming business throughout the state. A November trip netted orders for 28,675 cigars. By the middle of 1913, the promising business was prosperous enough to require a larger factory, and Hill decided to form a stock company, offering a capital stock of $25,000 divided into 1,250 shares with a par value of $20 per share. As the *Sarasota Times* put it, "Sarasota's businessmen have shown their faith in the future of this growing enterprise by subscribing liberally towards the stock." However, after the initial offering the reported shareholders were: J.H. Hill (84 shares); P.A. Hill (83 shares); J.K. Hill (83 shares); J.C. Hill (10 shares); and A.B. Edwards and H.L. Higel, two prominent locals (5 shares apiece). By the beginning of 1914, 30 others would pony up.

The company took on more help, employing nine men who rolled two thousand cigars a day and had difficulty keeping up with demand. Two more men were soon added.

Advertisements began appearing regularly in the *Sarasota Times*: "Try a SIMPATICA cigar. You'll like them. There isn't one man in fifty who finds fault with them; so they must be pretty good" and "You never see a butt of our cigars lying around, they are smoked as long as there's a whiff."

A pen and ink drawing of a smiling gentleman in a stiff wing collar and derby hat ran with the caption: "In order to make the most of yourself, smoke Sarasota Gems and you will feel right with your business and right with the world."

Thomas Riley Marshall, President Woodrow Wilson's vice president, had pronounced, "What this country needs is a really good five cent cigar." Heeding the call, Hill priced his brands at five cents and promised that they were equal in quality to the three-for-fifty-cent variety. Not only did they have a fine flavor, but his Havana Smoker also drew freely, burned evenly and held fire and ash. Hill said that his company used imported wrappers and only the best domestic tobacco for filler.

After 1916, Hill and his family left Sarasota and were lost to local history. But the cigar industry did not die with his departure. In the 1920s, Michael and Edward Roth began manufacturing cigars, "Havana's at 8 cents and up," in a "cigar factory and news stand." They later moved their operation to the Mira Mar Court, with a salesroom on Main Street where the El Prosito cigar was sold for a dime.

By this time, cigarettes had replaced the stogie as the smoke of choice. The admonition "Lips that touch tobacco will not touch mine" was mitigated by the fact that both sexes were puffing away. Philip Morris even sponsored a nationwide lecture tour for ladies on the etiquette of cigarette smoking, including such topics as how to hold a cigarette without looking affected—advice Hill's cigar-smoking railroad men never needed.

Passing the time in downtown Sarasota at the turn of the twentieth century. *Courtesy of the Sarasota County History Center.*

COUNTRY BOYS AND CITY BOYS

What did young people do for entertainment in the pioneer period of our history? Dave Broadway who came to town in 1893 and opened one of Sarasota's first restaurants, Broadway's, on the city pier, recalled, "Entertainment for fun-seekers here consisted solely of city boys fighting with country boys at a country dance. Or, country boys fighting with city boys at a city dance."

"MAY SARASOTA PROSPER"

When Sarasota voted to incorporate as a town in 1902, it chose as its motto the hopeful "May Sarasota Prosper." The town seal consisted of "a mullet with a rising sun over palmettos with shells at the base."

Lower Main Street, circa 1900. The water oaks were planted by Gillespie to spruce up the area. *Courtesy of the Sarasota County History Center.*

THE RIVIERA CITY

In trying to come up with a memorable nickname for Sarasota, *Sarasota Times* editor/publisher Rose Wilson noted that St. Augustine would always be saddled with the "Ancient City," which tied it forever to the past, and that Jacksonville had selected the "Gate City"—a wise choice. For Sarasota, she thought the suggestion of writer Robert C. Ginins of the "Riviera City" was a splendid choice. That section of southern France, he offered, was our only rival in beauty and climate. Rose wrote:

> *Suppose your city went forth blazoned as "Sarasota, the Riviera City," you can count the thousands upon thousands of cultured, wealthy and traveled people who will instantaneously respond to the magic word "Riviera."*

She further advised to take on the name before "any lesser community takes it for its own and deprives Sarasota of her surest name to win her laurels with."

A rugged-looking Sarasota as it was in the late 1880s. *Courtesy of the Sarasota County History Center.*

Over the years other appellations have applied: Sarasota, a City of Glorified Opportunity; Sarasota, the Seaside Town Favored by Nature; Sarasota, the Air-Conditioned City; Sarasota, a Land of Opportunities and Resources; Sarasota, the City of Homes.

A 1925 chamber of commerce brochure waxed poetic: "Sarasota County is a land of youthful hearts. Romance, beauty, the poetry of Nature's finest rhymes are synonymous with this land of Heart's Desire."

VERNONA FREEMAN AND OWEN BURNS

Vernona Freeman arrived in Sarasota in March 1912 with her relatives for a vacation. She was eighteen and beautiful, described in the paper as one of New York's most charming debutantes and a general favorite among Sarasota's younger set. When local developer Owen Burns met her, it was love at first sight.

By then, Burns was a major Sarasota landowner and was in the process of helping to lead the small community away from its fishing/agriculture roots toward its snowbird, resort-town future. He became a significant force in Sarasota's growth, particularly during the Roaring Twenties, and Vernona, his sweetheart, stood proudly by his side.

The two saw a great deal of each other during her visit, with Burns showing her the area and sharing his grand vision for its future. When she boarded the train to return home, the love-struck Burns spontaneously boarded with her.

While in New York, the two continued to court, and in what would become an ironic twist of fate, Burns proposed to her at high tea at the Ritz-Carlton Hotel. He then returned to Sarasota while wedding arrangements were finalized.

On June 4, 1912, the couple married in the home of Vernona's aunt and uncle, especially decorated for the occasion. The *Sarasota Times* reported from a New York paper that it was one of the prettiest weddings of the month. The lovely Vernona was dressed in white satin, her face was covered with an heirloom veil of point lace and a tulle veil extended to the end of her long train. She approached the altar on the arm of her uncle, who gave her away.

After the wedding, the couple set sail for a leisurely three-month tour of Europe. Upon their return to Sarasota, they were welcomed at the train station by Mayor Harry Higel, relatives, friends and the Sarasota Brass Band, which serenaded the group as they made their way to Burns's home on the bay for a reception.

During the next dozen years, Burns attended to his real estate/development businesses in slow-paced Sarasota, while Vernona ran their household, which was expanding with the birth of their children, five in all.

The 1920s real estate boom affected their lives dramatically. Owen, often pairing with John Ringling, was involved in all aspects of developing, dredging and building as Sarasota roared forward. And while he was constantly busy, he always found time to be home for supper with Vernona and the children. He was remembered by daughter Lillian as a loving husband and father who always managed to find time for his family.

The crowning glory of his work in Sarasota was the fabulous El Vernona Hotel, named to honor his loving wife. Its completion climaxed the whirlwind of his activity. When the storied hotel opened with grand fanfare on New Years Eve 1926, Owen and Vernona, then married for fourteen years, were toasted by the throng of well-wishers—how proud they must have felt!

The real estate crash followed shortly thereafter, and then the 1929 Depression.

The El Vernona was foreclosed and ultimately purchased by John Ringling, who changed its name to the John Ringling Hotel. When the building was demolished in 1998, it was to make way for a Ritz-Carlton, which completed the circle by opening the Vernona Restaurant.

Owen and Vernona remained married, weathering the hard times of the Great Depression with the same closeness that characterized their more affluent days. Owen died in 1937 and Vernona never remarried. She died in 1974. They are buried together in the family plot at Rosemary Cemetery.

THE SARASOTA YACHT AND AUTOMOBILE CLUB

When the new Sarasota Yacht and Automobile Club clubhouse was opened in January 1913, 250 people attended the grand party, played progressive

Ladies of the Woman's Club in costume for a colonial tea at the Sarasota Yacht and Automobile Club on Gulf Stream Avenue. *Courtesy of the Sarasota County History Center.*

500 (for which Dr. Joe Halton and George F. Chapline kept score), listened to music and danced the evening away. The paper reported that "the club house presented a scene of gay festivity, brightly illuminated with electric lights and Japanese lanterns; the national and club colors were draped over the doorway." E.C. Sourbrier won the progressive 500 and was awarded a handsome clock. Other prizes included cut glass, jewelry, silver and china.

Dr. Halton brought his chef, who prepared a supper of ham and turkey, sandwiches, salad, cake, ice cream and fruit punch. The grand march and dancing was led by new commodore Mr. Owen Burns and his wife. They tripped the light fantastic to the melodies of a three-piece string and piano orchestra, and the festivities lasted until 2:00 a.m.

The paper prophesized that the clubhouse would no doubt be the site of many such gatherings, but none would be more successful than this, the first.

Located on Gulf Stream Avenue, north of the city pier, the club was formed with thirty members for the purpose of promoting yachting and autoing. The initiation fee was fifty dollars, with annual dues of twenty-five dollars.

Ringling acquired the property in 1917, and in the 1920s it was remodeled into the Sunset Apartments, which were demolished in 1964.

THE SARASOTA KEY

A description of Longboat Key in the *Sarasota Times* on November 23, 1911, read as follows:

> *No more beautiful or favored spot exists on the Florida coast, for picturesque scenery, tropical surroundings and fertile soil.*
>
> *Rubber trees, growing wild, are found in large quantities, some magnificent specimens two to three feet through at the base and attaining a height of seventy-five feet.*
>
> *Sisal Hemp is found growing wild, so rank and in such quantities that it could be made a profitable industry.*
>
> *The Key is the natural home of the lime, the guava and the avocado pear. For years the limes and guavas have grown without care of cultivation, bearing for eight months the finest fruit to be found.*

An outing at Siesta Beach. *Courtesy of the Sarasota County History Center.*

About 18 families live on the Key, the majority of these having homesteads. Mr. Corey was the original settler, having spent fifteen years there, on his place, which now has the steamboat landing; about six years ago others became awake to the possibilities of Key property.

The farming potential on Siesta Key was a major selling point. When Harry L. Higel put together his brochure, *Siesta on the Gulf on Sarasota Key*, he noted:

The soil is extremely fertile and on account of the lack of frost, tomatoes, eggplants, peppers, cucumbers, strawberries, pineapples, beans, onions and other tender vegetables can be grown here and shipped during the months of December, January, February and March. It is also the natural home of the avocado, pear, guava, pineapple, lime, lemon, orange, grape-fruit and grapes.

Higel also saw the resort potential of Siesta and in 1913 built bathhouses for the day-trippers who came to Siesta by boat for swimming, picnics and fishing, offered refreshments and promised that "life lines, safety guards and all preventatives of accident will be provided."

To attract seasonal visitors, he opened the beautiful Higelhurst Hotel on Big Pass in 1915. He advertised: "Think of it! Living on a tropical island on Sarasota Bay where one can bathe in the waters of the Gulf of Mexico, hunt, fish, motor and enjoy life the year around."

Unfortunately the Higelhurst burned to the ground in 1917 and was never rebuilt. His son, Gordon Higel, longtime postmaster of Sarasota, recalled the aftermath of the fire:

> *I remember the morning it burned. He went out and I went out with him, and he had me by the hand and we went to the seawall* [on Gulf Stream Avenue]. *There in the distance was a dream that he had accomplished and here all of a sudden it's gone. And I can see him now. I looked up at him and tears were just coming down his cheeks. I was nine years old.*

Land Broker Baxter offered the following for sale:

> *AN ISLAND HOME. 4 acres on Little Sarasota Key with about 200 feet of nice high frontage on the bay. Nice 6 room house painted and furnished.*
> *Artesian water piped to the place. Fifty young fruit trees, nice oaks and cedars in front of the house. Good neighbors, Price $1000.*

THE DEATH OF "UNCLE" BEN STICKNEY

At the death of "Uncle" Ben Stickney, the gentleman for whom the Stickney Point Bridge and Stickney Point Road are named, Rose Wilson of the *Sarasota Times* was moved to write of the community's loss:

> *No news has brought greater sadness to Sarasota people than on Saturday, when a telephone message announced the sudden death of Uncle Ben Stickney, which occurred at his home on Sarasota Key, about 4 p.m.*
> *Willing hands at once made ready to go down to his home and to perform the last services and bring the body back to await instructions from his brother in New York.*
> *His frank and friendly manner and genial good nature carried sunshine wherever he went. No one on the bay was better known or counted his friends in greater numbers and every transient visitor, having once met Mr. Stickney,*

on returning to Sarasota, always enquired for and expressed a wish to again meet the cultured old gentleman, whose experience of the world was wide and whose views on life were broad; while among his friends, the sorrow felt for his loss is the greatest evidence of his worth.

A frequent visitor to town, "Uncle Ben" will be missed by all. Sadness falls on each one passing the old place, launches will glance in vain for the friendly salute. The house is closed and oppressive silence reigns, where for many years the happy voices of pleasure seekers made days of gladness; no more will his hearty grasp welcome the picnic parties to his domain, the gracious hospitality of his home, which was extended alike to friend and stranger, is now but a memory, and the murmuring waves along his shore breathe a requiem for the passing away of one who was loved and honored.

A SKATING RINK

On October 13, 1913, the young people of Sarasota were given something for their amusement when a skating rink opened on the second floor of the old schoolhouse on Main Street and Pine Avenue. A player piano provided music and the opening was a rousing success. It was reported that although most of the patrons were young,

many older ones go to look on, and quite a number of staid business men laid aside thoughts of values in real estate and the perplexities of mercantile life, and for the first time in years put on skates to find their skill of days long past had not been forgotten.

REGISTER GOES MISSING

On a warm September evening, S.M. Register, who rented a room over the T.C. Sines plumbing shop, went missing. He had prepared a meal but left it untouched on the small table, along with a note:

Sarasota, Fla., Sept. 13, 1913.
When this you see remember me, and you young men take warning from an old man. Drinking of whiskey and gambling have caused me to ruin.
Signed: S.M. Register.

BERTHA PALMER IS APPALLED

According to Bertha Palmer biographer Hope Black, when Palmer became aware of how poorly some locals were treating the African American laborers on her spread when she was away in Paris, she wrote to V.A. Saunders, who ran the local store at Osprey where the miscreants gathered:

Since buying at Osprey I have been greatly annoyed by the annual criminal assaults on my place and on my innocent, unprotected, sleeping Negroes by cowardly bands of armed men who come at night to shoot them up and drive them away. Every investor wants to know first about labor conditions and to be told of a community living back in the times and the atrocities of the lawless Ku Klux Klan era finishes its case at once.

In April 1914, she followed up with a letter to her manager, Albert Blackburn:

Dear Mr. Blackburn,

What prospective buyer would invest here after learning how I was treated? I who have spent a large amount of money to show what the soil and the climate can do and to create values...What horrid position I am forced into. It is disgusting. I should feel very badly to help put any man in the chain gang but perhaps it is our duty and thus make the country possible for honest, law-abiding citizens who are trying to develop it.

SCHOOL DAYS

The following were the books and curriculum for Sarasota High School in 1914:

Tenth-Grade Classes: *Lockwood and Emerson's Composition and Rhetoric*; Classics, to be supplied; Milne's *High School Algebra*; Myer's *General History*; Walker's *Caesar*; Houstor's *Physical Geography*.

Eleventh-Grade Classes: Halleck's *History of English Literature*; Classics, to be supplied; Wentworth's *Plain Geometry*; Allen & Greenough's *Six Oration Cicero*;

Carhart's & Chutes's *High School Physics*, revised edition; Myer's *General History*; Townsend's *Civic Government of the United States*; Fraser & Squair's *French Grammar*.

Twelfth-Grade Classes: Halleck's *History of American Literature*; Classics, to be supplied; Adams & Trant's *U.S. History*; Wentworth's *Plain Trigonometry*, (four months); Knox's Virgil, *Aeneid*; Brownlee & Fuller's *Chemistry*; Yocum's *Civil Government of Florida* (two months); Fraser & Squair's *French Grammar*.

Some curriculum!

POPULATION COUNT

At the end of 1914, the Woman's Club of Sarasota made house-to-house calls to obtain the city's population. Members counted 2,015 residents, noting that 43 babies were born that year and that the rate of infant mortality was very low. When Bertha Palmer arrived in town for a look-see in February 1910, the number was 840.

Lower Main Street, 1915, shortly after its frontier period and a few years before the 1920s real estate boom, which would transform it into a thriving snowbird paradise. *Courtesy of the Sarasota County History Center.*

A SALUBRIOUS CLIMATE

From its earliest years, Sarasota sold itself as a place where the ill and infirm could regain their health. The climate here was often described as salubrious. A brochure put out in the early 1910s noted that the temperature never exceeded ninety degrees and seldom fell below forty degrees. When the high was reached, it never lasted longer than an hour:

> *The Northern impression that the Florida summer is intensely hot is erroneous; they are by no means as exhaustive as the Northern summer. No sunstrokes occur here…The breezes from the Gulf arise every evening about dusk, and one is fanned gently to sleep, awaking in the morning feeling refreshed and invigorated.*

The *Sarasota Times* wrote that "many cures of invalids are reported here. Sarasota's climate [is] a marvelous boon to the afflicted." Noting that it could offer numerous examples of those who regained their health here,

Looking up lower Main Street from Palm Avenue toward Five Points, circa 1905. *Courtesy of the Sarasota County History Center.*

the paper told of Judge Goodhue of Alabama, whose heart trouble was improved "almost immediately."

In the same story, it was reported that a lady from Findlay, Ohio, who had arrived with limbs so badly swollen that she could not walk one hundred yards, could, within two weeks of her arrival, walk a mile; the swelling had disappeared and her heart problem was cured.

The paper enthused, "Sarasota is coming to be known as one of the most wonderful health resorts in all America." It prompted its readers to induce any of their family or friends to come down if they were experiencing heart trouble, bronchial trouble or asthma. "Our air and sunshine will do the rest, aided by plenteous supplies of distilled water."

In the 1920s, *This Week in Sarasota*, a boom-time weekly, headlined a story "Medicinal Value of Water From Springs Here Gives This Region Great Publicity" and noted that a gentleman named Jim Deboard, a manufacturer from Oskaloosa, Iowa, was sent to Sarasota at the insistence of his friend and was cured of Bright's disease, from which he suffered for fourteen years.

OFFENSES

Among the ordinances adopted by the town of Sarasota after the turn of the twentieth century was the following:

Offenses—Chastity, Public Decency, and Morality:
Section 1: Any woman whose reputation for chastity and virtue is bad, who shall be found on the streets plying her vocation or soliciting men, drinking, sitting on the streets, or in front of stores, or lounging at saloons, or conducting herself in a forward or improper manner, shall upon conviction, be fined not more than $50, or be imprisoned in the town jail not more than thirty days or both, at the discretion of the Court.

In the same vein, section 8 noted:

Any person, or persons, who shall occupy or allow to be occupied any bawdy house, or portion of a bawdy house, in the town, shall upon conviction thereof, pay a fine of not less that $10 for such services, collectable out of the owner or agent of the owner of such house, in case the same cannot be collected from the tenant or tenants upon execution.

THE SARA DE SOTA PAGEANT

Judge Jacob B. Chapline Sr. came to Sarasota in 1906 and immediately saw the area's potential. He and his son Jacob B. Chapline Jr. issued a comprehensive booklet extolling the virtues of the Sarasota Bay region "to induce people to come to the healthiest and most beautiful portion of Florida—Sarasota, on the west coast."

At the time of its publication, Chapline Sr. was the mayor of Sarasota and also sold real estate. In explaining the derivation of the lovely name "Sarasota" to his readers, another of the judge's sons, George Chapline, penned a "legend." He called it *Sarasota, The Beautiful* and in it sowed the seeds to what would become the basis of an annual weeklong celebration, the Sara de Sota pageant.

The tragic love story was first enacted in March 1916, with Genevieve Higel, daughter of early Siesta Key developer Harry Higel, playing Sara and J.B. Chapline Jr. playing the lustrous-eyed Chichi Okobee.

The pageant went on to become one of the premiere events in the South, drawing tens of thousands of out-of-towners. Initially held only sporadically, the junior chamber of commerce took over the event in 1935, and from then until 1957 it was the climax of our winter season, noted for its colorful Spanish-themed festivities, beauty pageant, frog Olympics, dances, parties and a grand parade, which showcased the wagons, performers and animals of the Ringling Bros. and Barnum & Bailey Circus.

CROSSING OVER

The antiseptic tone of today's obituary is a far cry from the finely crafted, inspirational prose that described yesteryear's crossing over the river. Those were the days when life was but "a slender thread."

C.V.S. Wilson, founder of the *Sarasota Times*, our first newspaper, informed readers of the passing of this fledgling community's members in heartfelt terms, with heavy doses of sentiment and an eye toward the Good Book. Death was referred to as "the coming of the messenger," "the final summons," "the dreamless night of long repose," "passing away," "crossing over" and "passing into the other world."

The elegized citizen was said to be of "sterling worth," "indulgent disposition," an "estimable gentleman" or "kindly gentlewoman," an "earnest Christian worker" or a "splendid young woman" or "aged matron."

This scene in Sarasota Bay is part of the first Sara de Sota celebration. *Courtesy of the Sarasota County History Center.*

These were the days after the turn of the twentieth century when no one in Sarasota was a stranger to another—each death was felt personally by all members of the community.

When the Reverend R.A. Seal died ("Brother Seal was always found on the right side of moral questions"), Sarasota was reminded of the impact of his loss on his family: "The old minister has fallen asleep after a long and useful life, leaving an aged wife, four children and several grandchildren to mourn his departure."

Similarly, Mrs. Harry Rigby left "a heart broken husband, and a grief stricken mother and father."

After Asa Chapline died of typhoid in 1911, the *Times* tried to soften the pain of his loss by assuring readers, "Although death was present, the calm serenity of his face robbed death of its terrors and he seemed to be at rest in peaceful sleep."

When F.B. Hagan crossed over, it was written of him: "His only fault—if he had faults—was a failure to properly appreciate his own worth and merit. He leaves the memory of an honored name—a monument more priceless than gold."

Asa was soon followed to his great reward by Judge J.B. Chapline, and Sarasotans were told of the judge's final hours: "As he felt life's declining days drawing to a close, he expressed himself ready to go and left for each of his family, fatherly counsel of Christian admonition." Shortly thereafter, "Like a shadow, softly and sweetly thrown from a passing cloud, Death fell upon him and the Judge was at rest."

Alfred P. Jones, who died in 1912, was remembered by the *Times* as "a good and kind neighbor who was strictly temperate in his habits, using neither liquor nor tobacco. He made little outward profession of Christianity, but he was a Christian at heart."

Captain Frank Guptil's death "cast a gloom over Osprey. If he had an enemy, it will be hard to find him."

An obit in 1914 noted that the decedent "had been drunk for a week and dies in that condition."

Few get to write their own obituaries. But C.V.S. Wilson's "goodbye" after he became too ill to run the paper could have served as his:

Now, with life's duties finished and only awaiting the call to pass over the River, I lay down my pen and pencil, put aside my stick and rule, vacate the editorial chair and walk out of the sanctum, with honor unsullied, aged seventy-three. Farwell.

He died eighteen days later.

When Rose took over the paper, she continued the tradition. She reported the sad end of Mrs. Fannie F., thirty-eight, the overworked, under-loved mother of four children who committed suicide by drinking a bottle of chloroform. Fannie had supported herself, the children and also one grown nephew who lived with her by taking in wash. The paper noted, "Her unfortunate habit of drinking made her subject to despondency." Earlier on the fateful day, she had told her neighbor of her plans to take her own life, but because she was drunk at the time, the threat was discounted. The children were sent to an orphanage.

When the two-year-old child of Mr. and Mrs. Collins died, Rose noted, "A gloom of sadness was cast over *The Times* office and in many homes, where the little boy was a great favorite."

At the death of little Dolly Yoemans, the eleven-year-old child of Mr. and Mrs. W.A. Yoemans, the paper addressed the angst of every parent:

Much interest had been centered in this little girl, whose long and serious illness had brought to the family the sympathy of every parent who could understand the anxiety and care with which they ministered to her needs and waited for the change that any day might bring, and always the fear that the shadow might fall; that the tiny ray of hope might be darkened in any moment by the wasting disease that for ten weary weeks had spent her little frame and sapped her strength.

At her funeral, the Reverend A.J. Beck assured the saddened congregation that she had passed to

a brighter world where there would always be the beckoning hands of little Dolly, to her loved ones, to the Home beyond where there is no sickness and no parting; the home of the Savior who, in love and tenderness, had said, "Let the little children come unto me."

Riding the Rails

The list of rich, famous and colorful characters who have breezed through Sarasota is very long and varied: Albert Einstein, Greta Garbo, Will Rogers, Jim Thorpe, Jack Dempsey, Eleanor Roosevelt, Lowell Thomas, Bob Hope, Prince Rainier, Jo Jo the Dog-Faced Boy and the list goes on.

The never-ending parade of personalities began arriving in February 1910, when Bertha Palmer, the era's society queen and America's answer to royalty, came by train from Chicago to check out the area.

Two years later, a gentleman who may have been the most interesting of them all presented himself at the office of Rose Wilson, editor/publisher of the *Sarasota Times*, to tell her his story.

It was on a bright Monday morning, April 8, 1912, that the well-dressed, impeccably groomed stranger introduced himself to Rose as "A–No. 1." The number one tramp in the world, that is; the king of the hobos.

He did not look the part.

He had come to Sarasota on Sunday evening, aboard the Seaboard Air Line Railway, hopping out of the boxcar when the train stopped at the downtown station at Lemon Avenue, where Mattison's is today.

Although this "boxcar tourist" arrived in overalls, he immediately changed into an impressive suit and, as was his custom when disembarking,

This picture of lower Main Street was taken from the De Soto Hotel. Notice the Methodist church at Five Points in the upper right; the belfry and steeple were added in 1906. *Courtesy of the Sarasota County History Center.*

THE SARASOTA TIMES

And Manatee County Advocate, Established 1886

DEVOTED TO THE WEST COAST OF MANATEE COUNTY.

VOL. XIII. No. 45.		SARASOTA. FLORIDA, THURSDAY, APRIL 11, 1912.			$1.00 A YEAR
AT REGULAR MEETING	**MEETING OF COUNTY SCHOOL BOARD**	**NOTED TRAMP VISITS TOWN**	**IMPROVEMENTS NOTED IN GROWING CITY**	**YACHT AND AUTO CLUB**	
COUNCIL ORDERS WATER PIPES ON STREETS CROSSING MAIN LINE TAKEN UP	Bradentown, Fla., Apr. 2, 1912. Board met with all members and Superintendent present. Minutes of last meeting were	"A NO. 1" AN EDUCATED WANDER ER TAKES IN SARASOTA ON TRIP THROUGH SOUTH	Highsmith & Prime will soon begin the erection of a brick ware-house, 30x60 feet south of the al-ley. In the rear of their Mai..	COMPLETE PLANS FOR THE EREC-TION OF A CLUB HOUSE ON BAY FRONT LOT	

The *Sarasota Times* reports that A–No. 1 had come to Sarasota. *Courtesy of the Sarasota County History Center.*

headed for the community's finest hotel; in those days of long ago, this was the Belle Haven Inn at Main Street and Gulf Stream Avenue.

As he strolled from the train station to the hotel, A–No. 1 passed by the *Sarasota Times* offices on the north side of lower Main Street. After a bath, a meal and a good night's sleep, he would call on the newspaper woman and proffer his bona fides as the king of tramps.

As Rose would learn, his credentials for the lofty claim were impressive. He had been tagged A–No. 1 in his youth by an elderly tramp who said to him, "Kid, you are all right, you're A–No. 1." Then, as the story goes, he was given the advice, "Never be seen in anyone's company with whom you would be ashamed to pass your mother's house in daylight."

The Early Years

His rail-riding life started in 1883, when he was eleven years old and ran away from home. As the years passed, wanderlust took hold of him and he could not stay still. By the time he arrived in Sarasota, he had been around the world three times and had amassed nearly 500,000 miles of ship and train travel—having spent, he said, a total of only $7.61 for transportation, making Arthur Frommer a spendthrift by comparison.

At each town from which he departed, he carved "A–No. 1" at the train station, along with an arrow pointing in the direction of his next journey.

His press clippings (Rose said they were dearer to him than gold) and calling cards of friends and acquaintances were impressive; they included Theodore Roosevelt, William Howard Taft, Thomas Edison and *Call of the Wild* author Jack London, whom A–No.1 had befriended and convinced to give up the life of a hobo in favor of writing. He also produced notes from high officials of every railroad in the country, all of which stated, "A–No. 1 is OK."

Rose seemed to have liked him. She reported that he was "well dressed and gentlemanly in appearance, and could pass for a prosperous business man." He did not smoke, drink or curse and spoke and wrote in four languages.

Among his newspaper clippings were stories of train accidents that he had prevented and an account of winning $1,000 from the *Police Gazette* for tramping to San Francisco from New York in eleven days and six hours. He told her that his tombstone would be inscribed: "A–No. 1, The Rambler, At Rest—At Last."

A–No. 1 was not poor. In fact, he was well-off financially, making a good living throughout his life by writing and publishing his adventures in books, which were sold at stores, newsstands and on trains throughout the country. It was reported in the *Hallettsville Herald* (Texas) that he was also an expert carver and whittler and obtained "favors" by carving intricate images on potatoes.

Rose did not know the colorful stranger's given name, saying of him, "But the mysterious man, whose identity has long since been lost to all but himself, without home, without friends, is not without aim." She told that he often encountered youngsters who had taken up, by choice or circumstance, the harsh hobo life and did his best to convince them to return to their homes, buying one-way tickets for them if they agreed to go back.

It is likely that, having told his story, A–No. 1 would have explored Sarasota for a day or two before changing back into his coveralls, carving his symbols at the train station and leaving on the next leg of his never-ending travels.

Interestingly, if he left town on Wednesday, he would have been aboard the same train that Bertha Palmer was taking back to Chicago. It's a nice thought: the king of tramps and the queen of society leaving Sarasota together—he in a boxcar, she in a private Pullman.

I learned (through *Wikipedia* of course) that A–No. 1 was born in San Francisco as Leon Ray Livingston. In 1973, Lee Marvin played him in the movie *Emperor of the North*, which was based on one of A–No. 1's books, *From Coast to Coast with Jack London*.

After a life on the rails the traveler died in 1944 at the age of seventy-two. A picture posted on the Internet shows his gravestone in the Laurel Hill Cemetery in Philadelphia, Pennsylvania. It is inscribed:

FATHER
Leon Ray Livingston
—"A No. 1"—
1872–1944

And although it does not say so, the rambling man is at rest at last.

TENT CITY

On Christmas morning 1913, it was announced that Sarasota, à la Coronado Island in San Diego, was going to be the home of a tent city on Siesta Key. Initially, ten tents were going to be raised and managed by Mrs. Fannie Van Eyck. The tents were to be waterproof and stretched over a wooden frame, "so built and braced that it would take a gale sufficient to wreck a frame house to do them any damage." The *Times* report continued, "Fortunately this part of Uncle Sam's domain is singularly free from any such storms, and offers exceptional advantages for camp life close to salt water."

Mrs. Van Eyck had managed a hotel in Atlantic City, and the Siesta Key setup was described as a "new and attractive method of outdoor living in Florida."

A TOAST TO GILLESPIE

At a testimonial banquet for John Hamilton Gillespie, held at the Sarasota Yacht and Automobile Club on March 10, 1913, thirty club members came together to pay homage and give thanks to the great man for his "public spirited, generous contributions to the general welfare." Toastmaster Rube Allyn, publisher of the *Sarasota Sun*, lauded Gillespie, and toast after toast was made with "rousing oratory."

The dinner spread included celery hearts, queen olives, clam chowder, grilled pompano with lemon butter sauce, potatoes julienne, roast young chicken stuffed with oysters, black currant jelly, mashed potatoes, green peas and stone crab salad.

It was said that the festive evening

> *developed sentiments of devotion to the up building of Sarasota, and a determination to eliminate factional disputes and misunderstandings so that a kindly spirit of good fellowship would be a noticeable characteristic of the city.*

No doubt this referred to the bad blood that had developed between Harry Higel and Gillespie, which the celebration helped to ameliorate.

COLONEL REED'S CATCH

It was reported in J.B. Chapline's early promotional brochure about Sarasota that Colonel H.V. Reed of Chicago, "in two months of fishing, caught by himself with hook and line, in Sarasota Bay, thirty hundred fish of thirty-four different varieties." He reportedly had come to Sarasota for his health and was advised by his doctor to spend as much time near the water as he could.

MAKING A LIVING

A brochure put out by the Sarasota-Venice Company in 1915 assured readers that someone wishing to make a new start in the area could do so for $1,247 and itemized the costs as follows:

> *temporary house and furnishings $600*
> *five-acre clearing $200*
> *fence, all of one side, half of 3 sides $112*

rim ditch, half of 3 sides, varies with special conditions, about $50
70-foot two-inch well $35
horse and tools $250

And after you arrived, it was very cheap to live. One could easily grow his own food, hunt for game, fish and raise poultry. Wood for fuel was readily available and only lightweight clothing was necessary. "An energetic worker, even without experience, can be practically certain of success with $2,000 in money." The brochure noted that nearly all of the residents of this district came here with practically nothing, and "a failure here is comparatively unknown."

A testimonial from C.M. Robinson underscored the potential for a hardworking person to make a go of it in Sarasota:

If a man can't make a living here he can't make it anywhere. I ran away from a ship in Key West and came here and I have made good. If they'd work here as they have to in Georgia and Alabama they'd all get rich. It is the easiest country to make a living and the easiest to get ahead.

AMENITIES

By 1915, the slowly growing community, which had achieved a great deal of publicity with the coming of Bertha Palmer in 1910, could brag that it had the following amenities: the Sarasota Yacht and Automobile Club; a Woman's Club; a board of trade; an eighteen-hole golf course; tennis and card clubs; two picture theatres; a city band; an ice plant; a telephone system with three hundred phones on the local exchange; a new all-brick school building with ten teachers; two weekly newspapers; two banks; ten hotels (one all-brick fireproof structure that wouldn't burn to the ground until the next year); plus numerous boardinghouses and churches.

SARASOTA'S GARDEN SPOT

An early forerunner of today's modern housing developments, laid out on a fifty-six-acre tract complete with bay views, a clubhouse, a private yacht basin and social amenities, was platted by Katherine Elizabeth McClellan of Massachusetts and marketed by her and her sister, Daisietta "Miss Daisy" McClellan.

These daughters of a wealthy physician were world travelers before Katherine discovered Sarasota in 1903. Miss Daisy and their mother followed a few years later, searching, as had so many others, for the healthful climate that Sarasota provided.

In those days, Sarasota Bay was in clear sight from practically everywhere in McClellan Park. Katherine, who was an accomplished photographer with an artist's eye for beauty, put together a sales brochure showcasing the superlative water views. She christened their development "Sarasota's Garden Spot" and, in March 1916, offered lots for $800 to $2,500, with cement sidewalks, running water and septic tanks. As their ad put it, "If you are a lover of beauty, don't miss seeing McClellan Park."

Rose Wilson noted in the *Sarasota Times* that substantial improvements had been made to the property by the sisters—"a fine compliment to the ability of Miss McClelland and her sister, Miss Daisy"—and heralded their effort as "a distinct advantage to Sarasota which someone remarked would 'be the beginning of a Palm Beach for the West Coast.'"

After a year of clearing and beautifying their property, the sisters planned a suitably grand opening celebration to kick off their sales campaign, including a tennis tournament, an afternoon tea, an evening reception and a dance ending at midnight with the revelers singing "Auld Lang Syne."

The next year, management of the development was taken over by Howard Elliott, who reduced the price of the property to a range more in keeping with the World War I economic realities of the time: $450 to $900 per lot.

The sisters, who never married, pursued other interests, traveling abroad for a time and then returning to open a tearoom and gift shop in what would later become McClellan Park School. Katherine became ill and died in 1934. Miss Daisy, as she was forever and affectionately known, died on February 16, 1952. She was eighty-four.

"WILDCATS WERE ALWAYS A PROBLEM"

In recalling the dangers faced by the homesteading settlers, Jasper Crowley wrote:

Wildcats were always a problem. Sometime so common the dogs failed to bark at them. Mother would see them come over the fence, grab a chicken and be gone…Every child was afraid of a wildcat and sooner or later expected to be caught by one. One morning we got up and mother was gone, we soon found out mother had seen a wildcat go into the cane patch so she went into the cane patch to run him out so dad could shoot him. We never expected to see mother again.

OCEAN DEEP AND "BIG DADDY"

Ocean Boulevard on Siesta Key is named for Ocean Deep Hansen Roberts, wife of Captain Louis "Big Daddy" Roberts who, with Harry Higel and E.M. Arborgast, platted the north end of Sarasota Key as Siesta on the Gulf. Susan Roberts Spears recalled in her book *Assorted Tales and Other Lies* that five of Ocean and Louis's twelve children died in one week from food poisoning and that after Ocean buried them, her two-year-old in the arms of an older child, she was never the same.

Captain Roberts opened the Siesta Inn Hotel in 1906, and during the 1920s his Roberts Casino at the intersection of Beach Road and Ocean Boulevard could entertain as many as three thousand guests at one time. The

Catches like this were common, and fishing was one of Sarasota's earliest tourist draws. *Courtesy of the Sarasota County History Center.*

casino offered "all the joys of surf bathing or fresh water bathing...where one may receive the fullest effects of the sun's curative rays." It was razed in 1957 to make way for an apartment building.

BIRD KEY MANSION

So beautiful was the Bird Key mansion, which Thomas W. Worcester built for his wife Davie, that when it was first opened to visitors the *Sarasota Times* noted:

> *The conventional rule of etiquette taught from childhood that one should not appear to take notice or make comments in a strange house was completely cast aside, all the guests were frankly and even loudly outspoken in exclamations of delight and sincere admiration as they passed from room to room.*

Sadly, by that time Mrs. Worcester, who wanted it for her retirement home, had died.

A WAR MEMORIAL

A refreshing sense of sentiment characterized yesterday's Sarasota, obvious especially in the memorials built to honor the local soldiers, sailors and marines who served their country.

The soft spot for our armed forces extends to the early days of our involvement in World War I.

The first group of Sarasotans, more than fifty of Sarasota's U.S. Naval Militia, left for the battles in Europe on Easter Sunday, April 8, 1917, and within the small community, their presence would be greatly missed.

At the Virginian Theatre on upper Main Street, a multidenominational church service was held for them, and when it was over, a large number of the citizenry turned out to the Seaboard Air Line train station to wave their "sailor lads" goodbye and wish them well.

It was a stormy day, and the *Sarasota Times* noted that "rain mingled with the tears that were shed" for these boys, "the flower of this city."

Even before the war ended, the appreciative community took up a collection to honor them by erecting a flagpole in the center of Five Points. Bertha Palmer donated a large stars and stripes that would proudly fly from it, and on a bright Saturday afternoon, June 23, 1917, it was dedicated in what was described as an inspiring and impressive ceremony.

The flag was carried to the site by fifteen members of the Red Cross auxiliary dressed in nurses' uniforms. They were followed by the Patriotic Young Girl's organization, outfitted in middy blouses, white skirts and sailor hats.

Along the route they stopped occasionally to perform various military drills to the delight of the crowd, which lined both sides of Main Street. Their maneuvers "brought forth hearty applause," according to the paper.

Five Points was a symbolic setting for the flagpole. It was the heart of the community, the very spot from which the town had been platted, and for many years was the focal point of downtown. Passers-by looked daily to the stars and stripes and thought of the sacrifice that was made. A Boy Scout troop was put in charge of raising and lowering the flag daily.

When the "patriotic young men" came home after the war, Sarasota was awash with excitement. No one had been killed in battle, and inscribed in the center of the street near the flagpole, in large letters, were the words "Welcome Buddies."

THE VELVET HIGHWAY

The road to Venice was completed in 1918 as part of a $250,000 bond issue to build thirty-four miles of hard-surfaced roads between Sarasota, Venice, Bee Ridge and Fruitville, all small communities in Manatee County. The laborious task was made easier by the newly patented cutting plow designed by African American inventor Henry C. Webb of Bradenton. It facilitated the removal of thick palmetto growth, which previously had to be removed by hand and a grubbing hoe.

Describing the work involved, A.K. Whitaker, in *One Man's Family*, wrote:

Up at five—breakfast—clean up camp—at work by seven—a sandwich for lunch—work until five—a bath in a nearby creek—supper—by dark into bed under mosquito bars to keep from being eaten alive.

Although the road was only nine feet wide, requiring an oncoming vehicle to pull off to allow the other to pass by, it was a vast improvement and was dubbed the "Velvet Highway."

THE 1920s

When the boom was at its peak here there were stacks of checks by every cash register, smiles on every face, money in every pocket, people in every house, all business houses and stores occupied and the people bought everything they could find to buy.

They'd buy real estate in the morning and sell at a profit in the afternoon. A piece of property would change hands four or five times through purchase of a contract before anybody could find time to get an abstract.

Fortune hunters came from all parts of the country to buy acreage for subdivision purposes. They gave no thought to drainage, utilities or other improvements. They would have a plat made up, file at the courthouse and put the lots on the market for sale. They laid out four lots to the acre and would sell off each of these lots for a price originally paid for the acre, and they left the city holding the bag as far as any improvements were concerned.

Some of the subdivisions were under water; some had an underlying hard pan while others were too far removed from the center of activity to warrant their existence. Some of these subdivisions platted in 1925 were sold as acreage in 1957.

—*Roger Flory, real estate man, civic leader and longtime Sarasota booster*

THE LAND OF GLORIFIED OPPORTUNITY

Sarasota was awash with optimism in the 1920s as the community evolved from a backwater town to a full-fledged city. Growth was rampant and the old made way for the new. When the antiquated Belle Haven Hotel, built

A map of the Sunshine State in 1921. "Come on down." *Courtesy of the Sarasota County History Center.*

The 1920s

as the De Soto Hotel by John Hamilton Gillespie, was set to be razed, the *Sarasota Herald* intoned "Local Landmark Doomed," but there was no call to save it. In its place would be built the skyscraper American National Bank building, a symbol of the emerging Sarasota.

Everywhere you cared to look, construction was taking place. The larger buildings included the Hotel Sara Sota at Main and Palm (credited with being Sarasota's first skyscraper), the First Bank and Trust at Five Points, Charles Ringling's Sarasota Terrace Hotel east of town, Owen Burns's El Vernona on what had been Banana Avenue (changed to the more with-it sounding Broadway Avenue) and the Mira Mar Apartments and Hotel on Palm Avenue.

The needs of the thousands of newcomers necessitated the building of new churches, schools, housing developments, retail shops, theatres, restaurants, roads, bridges, banks, hotels, apartments and rooming houses.

As each community in Florida fought for its fair share of newcomers who were pouring into the state, the Sarasota Chamber of Commerce, formerly

Sarasota's premier hotel during the 1920s boom and beyond was Owen Burns's El Vernona, later the John Ringling Hotel and finally the John Ringling Towers. Burns's adjacent office building would become the retirement home of Karl and Maderia Bickel. Both structures were demolished to make way for the Ritz-Carlton Hotel. *Courtesy of the Sarasota County History Center.*

the board of trade, was active in siphoning as many as it could into what was being billed as "the Land of Glorified Opportunity."

The chamber's 1925–26 brochure described Sarasota County as follows:

It was in the gladness of His dreams that God fashioned the earth and flung it from the hollow of His hand through myriad meteors and the shimmering tracery of the stars. It must have been that he lingered over the effect to be produced in Sarasota County, and for all these years Nature seemed to have rested in raptured contemplation of her rich and varied charms.

There was more:

Sarasota County is transcendent with charm; her resources seem interminable. The beauty of scenery, varied and fascinating, is an inspiration. Aureate glory is everywhere—in the sea, in the dales, forested isles and leafy clusters and bouquets of greenery, with phantom flecks of dainty color, and with vistas blue with haze of distance-dream fully dim and cool and mystical.

Wow! What a place.

And there was more. There were no "undesirables" afoot in this idyllic community. The chamber promised:

You'll see no drunkenness on our streets, and you can recourse to the police blotter of Sarasota and see that there are no robberies, no highway attacks, and possibly the loss of only two automobiles in a year's time… We will not build up Sarasota at the expense of the undesirable element. The Sarasota of tomorrow will feel the elevating influence of Sarasota of today.

MURDER MOST FOUL ON SIESTA KEY

He was bludgeoned so horribly that he was unrecognizable, his face and head a bloody pulp. His crumbled body was left lying and dying on a sandy beach road on Siesta Key.

Bert Luzier and his son, Merle, on the key to gather a truck full of shell, came upon him at 8:30 on the morning of January 6, 1921. They thought a car had hit him, that someone barreling along lost control, ran him down and left the scene.

They had no idea who he was. His head was split open on the right side just above the eye, leaving a two-inch gap in his skull, and the left side was badly crushed, with several bad wounds on the back of his head. He was lying facedown in blood.

The Luziers gathered up the battered body as gently as they could and slid him into the cab of their truck. Sarasota did not yet have a hospital, so the Luziers hurried him over the narrow road to Dr. Joseph Halton's house in town.

It took only a cursory exam for Halton to know that he did not have the wherewithal at his home to offer proper medical assistance. Halton had the Luziers proceed to the Thacker undertaking parlor just down the street. There he could dress the wounds and prepare the body for transport to the hospital in Tampa, fifty-five miles away. The identity of the injured man was still unknown.

While Dr. Joe was treating him at Thacker's, he was shocked to discover that the badly mauled body belonged to Harry L. Higel, one of Sarasota's most prominent citizens. It was also determined that the former mayor, councilman, businessman, developer and Sarasota booster had not been run down but had been the victim of a brutal beating with a club or some other heavy instrument.

The decision to stabilize Higel, take him by car to Bradentown, twelve miles away over poor roads, and there make a connection with the northbound train was a long shot. Dr. Halton must have known that the chances for his friend's survival were slim. But this was Harry Higel, and everything humanly possible had to be tried. Higel was as synonymous with Sarasota as the sun and sand.

Sarasota had a population at that time of a couple thousand people. The land boom that would transform the community (and the state) into a winter playground for northern snowbirds was a few years away. In 1921, everyone in Sarasota knew everyone else and knew them well. Higel was a standout, one of a handful of progressives who were pushing the community toward its destiny, men who saw in the virginal beauty and temperate climate of the area the surefire ingredients of a resort second to none.

Higel had come to the area from Philadelphia in 1884 with his parents and brothers. The family settled in Venice, but Harry made his way farther north and became involved in the affairs of Sarasota. In the course of his career he dabbled in shipping, selling real estate, development and was a three-term mayor and seven-term councilman. He was a dynamo, and he was liked and respected.

Higel turned his attention to Sarasota Key, a pristine tropical paradise reachable only by boat. On the north end of the key he and two acquaintances, Captain Louis Roberts and E.M. Arbogast, platted Siesta on the Gulf and began developing it "along the lines that appeal to the well-to-do who wish to leave the snows…and get down here for five or six months of continuous good weather."

Canals were dug, forming Bayou Louise, Bayou Hanson and Bayou Nettie, and in 1913 Higel opened bathhouses for day-trippers who came to Siesta by boat for swimming, picnics and fishing.

In 1915, he produced a brochure showcasing the idyllic life that was available in this offshore paradise: "Think of it! Living on a tropical island on Sarasota Bay where one can bathe in the waters of the Gulf of Mexico, hunt, fish, motor and enjoy life the year around."

He opened the Higelhurst Hotel that year on beautiful Big Pass. It was two stories tall, with columns all around and a large screened porch on the second floor. Two hundred guests were ferried over for the grand-opening celebration.

The sheriff was notified of the horrific crime and came to the site to look for clues. Robbery was discounted as nothing was taken—his wallet, watch and other valuables were still on his person. Bloodhounds were called out.

The *Sarasota Times* reported that Rube Allyn, former editor of the *Sarasota Sun* and then current editor of the *Florida Fisherman*, was arrested by Chief Deputy Sheriff Brown.

Higel and Allyn had been feuding for quite some time, but the evidence against Allyn was circumstantial.

> *It is known that Mr. Allyn arrived in the city last night and that he was carried out to the Siesta Bridge in an auto. Parties taking him to the bridge state that he complained of being in a depressed mood, the depression being so acute, he stated, that he decided he had better give up his work for a few days and come home.*

The paper noted:

> *The web of circumstantial evidence that is woven around Mr. Rube Allyn…inclines many to believe he is the one but we can only withhold opinion until*

*the charges are proven. For the wife and children of the accused man we can
not but feel sympathy for their lot is one of hardship and sorrow.*

For Higel's funeral, the *Sarasota Times* headlined "Remains of Harry L.
Higel Laid to Rest with Imposing Ceremonies" and described the burial
procession as one of the largest ever known in Sarasota, marching from
the city hall building at the foot of lower Main Street to Five Points, then
to Mango Avenue and on to Rosemary Cemetery. The Antinarelli band, in
town for an engagement, led the funeral procession.

Allyn denied guilt, and for his safety he was spirited away to Bradentown
and jailed there. A coroner's jury met and determined that there was enough
evidence to hold him for the murder.

He remained incarcerated for sixty-one days until the grand jury of
Manatee County found that there was not sufficient evidence to warrant a
true bill. He was released on March 9, 1921.

In August of that year, a $1,000 reward was offered for the arrest and
conviction of the person who committed what was being called "one of the
foulest crimes in the history of this section."

The brutal murder of Harry Higel remains a mystery.

RAILROADS, STEAMSHIPS AND AUTOMOBILES

The traditional means of transport to Florida at the turn of the twentieth
century—the railroads and steamships of Henry Flagler on the east coast
and Henry Plant on the west coast—offered the ultimate in comfort and
traveling ease.

Sophisticated brochures published by Flagler's Florida East Coast
Railway and Plant's the Plant System showcased majestic hotels, towns
and points of interest and recreational activities that could be found at
every stop.

By the time of the 1920s Florida real estate boom, Henry Ford's Model-T
"Flivver" had opened new vistas to the masses, enabling hundreds of thousands
to come to Florida. The early cars were often cantankerous and had the
comfort factor of a buckboard wagon. Their hand-crank starters broke many
a wrist and arm, and protection from the elements was not a strong suit.

Early roads were better suited to horses, especially after rainstorms.
Blowouts were common. Dry days produced dry roads and billowing

clouds of irritating dust. Wet days produced muck and deep ruts. It was not uncommon to see a motoring tourist being pulled out of the mire by a farmer and his mule.

Making the journey from the Northeast to and through the Sunshine State was a long and sometimes arduous adventure, particularly before the Dixie Highway, called "the string upon which Florida has strung her jewels," and later the Tamiami Trail were completed.

But in spite of the difficulty inherent in early auto travel, it was the transport of necessity for many who could not otherwise afford to come down for a look-see and join in the hoopla. In fact, so many were migrating south that it was said that "Florida highways have been black with a stream of automobiles"—a reference to the black Model-T.

As county roads improved, they became sources of pride, touted for the speed and ease with which they could be traversed, the surrounding scenic beauty and an indicator that a community was prospering.

Train travel also increased dramatically as the 1920s shot forward. During this era of "Coolidge prosperity," more money was available to more people who wanted to ape the bluebloods, if only just for the length of time of an annual vacation. Being a guest on a private yacht may have been out of the question but a ticket on a Pullman was not, nor was the destination of choice—Florida.

"THE SOMEWHAT PREVALENT PRACTICE OF MASHING"

As the good times rolled on, a miscreant or two managed to slip across the border into our fair county, and fearing for the well-being of the fairer sex, Mayor Everett J. Bacon instructed the city police department to jail male mashers. He ordered Sarasota's finest to patrol the city streets throughout the day and night "in an effort to put a stop once and for all time to the somewhat prevalent practice of mashing." The mayor promised that the "sheiks" who were annoying women on the streets of Sarasota would be arrested.

The paper reported on the crackdown:

> *Recently two Bradenton youths were arrested here on a warrant sworn out by a local man who accuses them of approaching his wife on the street and attempting to engage her in a conversation, almost forcing the woman into an automobile parked along the curb awaiting a victim.*

The 1920s

The *Sarasota Herald* assured its readers that, as in the big cities where such shenanigans were occurring, "heavy fines and jail sentences" would put an end to the problem.

A front-page editorial in the *Sarasota Herald* on August 8, 1926, read:

> SHOOT THEM ON THE SPOT. *We have received a copy of a letter sent by a prominent citizen to the mayor in reference to the fact that his wife was grossly insulted by two men in a car the other evening as she was returning home from the theatre about 10 o'clock. Any man who will insult a woman on the street deserves to be shot on the spot. We have never carried a gun, but we believe we shall get one and be prepared to use it on the first justification on any brute who we find molesting women after this fashion. If the city authorities cannot, or will not, clean out these dirty whelps, who prowl around the streets in motor cars seeking opportunity to insult our women folk, it behooves us men to go after the situation. It has to be stopped. We advise every man to buy a gun for his wife or daughter and give them lessons in the use of it. If a few of these miscreants can be shot, perhaps the practice of molesting women on the streets of Sarasota will become too dangerous for these contemptible and cowardly scoundrels to indulge in it.*

S. Tilden Davis, the chief of police, let it be known that he would not tolerate drunks walking the city streets, giving special attention to those found wandering around in an inebriated state on the Sabbath. Davis noted that though a man could not be termed a drunk with only a few drinks under his belt, if "he gave the least indication that he was not in full control of his powers of speech and locomotion," he would be jailed.

The *Sarasota Herald* reported that the current city jail was not large enough to deal with the new element making its way into Sarasota during these wild, Roaring Twenties days and stated that a new slammer was needed as soon as possible.

BOLSHEVIK AMUSEMENT

In April 1926, Dr. E.J. Bulgin, revivalist preacher, came to Sarasota and took to task the parents of Sarasota's flaming youth, condemning "the modern flapper and her sheik, and all forms of jazz as 'Bolshevik amusement.'" He likened modern parents with those of biblical times

73

who allowed their children to stray and meet with trouble and disaster, both physical and spiritual.

As for the problem with drinking during this time of Prohibition, the good reverend proclaimed, "If every pair of pants was filled with a real man instead of simply an imitation, booze could be wiped out in a week's time. I believe in liberty but not in liberties."

Police Chief Davis took umbrage at Dr. Bulgin's remarks during one of his revival meetings that the chief and other officers were "either in cahoots with the law-breaking elements or are inefficient in their duties." The chief also took exception to Bulgin's remark that "on every corner of the city, liquor can be smelled."

Not being dissuaded, the preacher refused to recant and asserted that his charges could be proved.

Booze and Guns

After a shooting at a downtown hotel involving gamblers, the *Sarasota Herald* had had quite enough of the lawlessness that had recently increased in staid Sarasota. On January 1, 1927, the paper editorialized:

> *Booze And Guns. As long as men drink booze and tote guns, there is a strong probability of bloodshed. That is just what has happened in this city. A gun in the hand of a drunken man has sent another man to the hospital and probably the grave. Mixed up with the booze and guns is gambling. Gambling usually gathers gamblers, or creates them, and gamblers are not good citizens. Any community in which they are permitted to carry on their activity soon becomes infested with bad men and dissolute women...If we are going to make it possible for the booze guzzling, gambling and prostitute fraternities to find a soft berth in Sarasota we shall soon gain an unenviable reputation that will put a crimp in the fair name which this city has as a winter resort...The time has come to clean up and keep clean.*

Of the three thousand voters who registered to vote in the county elections of June 1926, one person marked an *x* after Prohibition Party. County supervisor of registrations R.B. Chadwick refused to name the surviving member of the party, saying that it was "but fair to afford protection to any man who could hold out against 2,999 others."

The 1920s

THE WRECK OF A PADDLE-WHEELER

Frank Archibald, the son of Sarasota developer and pioneer merchant Ira Graham Archibald, recalled that when a canal was dredged on Siesta Key to form Palm Island in 1923, the wreck of a paddle-wheel steamer was found. He conjectured that it had been washed ashore during a hurricane or perhaps sunk trying to get through a pass. "There were skeletons of people aboard with gold rings on their fingers."

The younger Archibald, a major developer on Siesta Key, also recalled that it was he who accidentally knocked down the old watering trough at Five Points when he hit it with his "old man's Ford."

GILLESPIE PARK

In 1924 Owen Burns, in a show of civic responsibility, offered to sell the city council a ten-acre tract of land to be used only for a park that would be named "Gillespie Park" to honor Sarasota's first mayor. The price was set at $30,200, one that the *Sarasota Times* called well below the actual value. Burns, knowing that the council did not have this amount of money, said it could be paid "when ever possible." Burns was quoted:

> *Gentlemen, I am doing this as a civic proposition. Ever since the death of Col. Gillespie I have been anxious to see a park somewhere in the city, which would be named after him, and in which a beautiful monument to his memory could be erected.*

The park is still in use today. However, no statue of Colonel Gillespie has ever been erected there.

THE DEATH OF CHIVALRY

Noting a change for worse in manners vis-à-vis men toward women, the *Herald* reprinted an editorial that ran in the *Hardee County Herald*:

> *The accusation is made that men no longer are as courteous to women as they once were. Good manners are out of date, it is said. The change is*

imputed to the change in woman's status. Since she has left the shelter of the home and engaged in business and public activities, it is not considered needful to show her deference. Men, unashamed, will remain seated in street cars while women stand; they will smoke in mixed society, without so much as asking permission; they will speak of girls as "fellows," "She's a good fellow" one will hear them say. Does it mean that the enfranchisement of women, the striking of the shackles, has killed chivalry? That men cannot be expected to show courtesy to women unless women occupy a subordinate position in society?

It may be that women are themselves partly to blame. A few foolish ones dislike to be thought of as the "weaker sex" or "the gentler sex" and on that account discourage the showing of deference to them, thinking it implies that they are not the equals of men. Of course they are not the equals of men in muscular strength, and they should glory in not being the equals of men in coarseness, either.

The Out-of-Door School

One of the most progressive and highly regarded schools in this country was established in Sarasota in 1924 by Miss Fanneal Harrison with the assistance of Miss Catherine Gavin, two women who had dedicated their lives to the welfare of the youth of the world.

They opened the Out-of-Door School with the ideal of offering a "place where the physical, mental and spiritual development of the child may be normal and joyous." Or, as a poem by one of its first students put it, "Going to school under the blue skies, makes a child healthy, happy and wise."

The ladies had seen the opposite side of that coin during their years in Europe, through and after the great calamity of World War I that had left so many homeless and much of Europe suffering from illness, disease and hunger.

While nurturing the suffering of Europe, they discovered the Decroly method of teaching. Devised by Dr. Ovide Decroly, a Belgian physician, psychologist and educator, the method proposed "helping children to find out what they themselves want to know."

Fanneal received two years of medical training at the University of Michigan before going to Europe, where she organized and directed health camps for undernourished children in France. She became a director of the Czechoslovakia Junior Red Cross and was later a member of Herbert Hoover's Peace Mission to Europe.

Catherine, her co-director, brought five years of experience with the Girls Club camps and Camp Fire Girls groups, plus two years of reconstruction work in war-torn France and Belgium.

Both women's unselfish efforts were lauded by the governments of Belgium, Czechoslovakia, France and America.

They began the school with three open-air buildings on three acres on Siesta Key. Ten students made up the initial enrollment. An early school brochure noted the teaching atmosphere at Out-of-Door School: "These teachers are not forcing children what grown-ups think the children ought to know; they are helping the children to find out what the children themselves want to know."

Progress reports were comprehensive and individually tailored to each student, including physical development (noting changes in height and weight) and hand-written accomplishments in an eclectic range of subjects: sports, music, art, crafts, grammar, reading, arithmetic, music, geography, science and social and ethical development. It was reported of one student, "His sunny disposition and his exuberant expressions of delight over daily happenings were quite refreshing."

Miss Harrison retired in 1939. She lived out the remainder of her years in a nursing home and passed away on December 23, 1973. She was ninety-two.

SPRING TRAINING LITTLE NAPOLEON STYLE

The juggernaut New York Giants, with firebrand John J. McGraw at the helm, was one of the best teams in the Major Leagues; a powerhouse that won the World Series in 1921 and 1922 and the National League Pennant in 1923. During the Golden Age of Sports, a time when baseball was truly America's favorite pastime, avidly followed throughout the nation, McGraw was one of the most readily known names in the sports world.

John Ringling, with his many New York connections (he was a major stockholder in Madison Square Garden, where his circus opened its season each year), was credited with scoring the Giants. The paper enthused that if the Giants made Sarasota their permanent training home, "there should be a monument erected at Five Points with John Ringling on one side and John McGraw (who yielded to the importunities of Mr. Ringling) on the other."

The Giants stayed for only four seasons and there is no monument at Five Points.

Mighty McGraw got caught up in what seemed like easy money in local real estate. By the end of 1925, he lent his name and reputation (polished to a bright sheen) to one of the most ballyhooed projects of the era—Pennant Park subdivision, "One of the Most Beautiful Bits of Homeland in the World."

McGraw had been a roughhouse player and was a firebrand manager. His antics were well reported up North, but locally he was portrayed as a gentleman of sterling character, the "Roosevelt of Sport—Clean, Honorable, Trustworthy—A Winner."

One advertisement solemnly proclaimed, "There isn't a man who has ever been admitted to John J. McGraw's friendship who wouldn't walk across the brimstone pit on a rotten rail to serve him." His abrasive personality traits were not conducive to salesmanship.

On December 18, 1925, the banner headline for the *Sarasota Daily Times* announced "395 Acres, Cost $987,500, Added to Pennant Park." That brought the development's size up to 1,451 acres, "one of the best and biggest developments in the state." The development was said to have five thousand lots and was advertised throughout the country with real estate offices in the major cities.

The list of Sarasotans who bought homesites in Pennant Park included many of the town's movers and shakers: J.H. Lord, A.B. Edwards, the Paynes, Ralph C. Caples, Charles Ringling and numerous others. The mayors of Bradenton and Palmetto were said to be among the buyers. As it was situated between Sarasota and Bradenton, the development was hawked there as well, and according to the paper, "The people of Bradenton have taken to Pennant Park like a parrot to sunflower seeds." McGraw began to be cited in the *Sarasota Herald* as "the well known realtor" and a "realtor and sportsman."

After the hurricane of September 1926, however, the boom began to peter out. For places like Pennant Park, the party was over. By the end of that year, the deleterious effects of the real estate bust were being felt throughout the community. Instead of glowing accounts of Sarasota's rosy future, the news was of mortgage foreclosures, bankruptcies, suits and countersuits—from the prospective of today's real estate debacle, it sounds all too familiar.

The 1920s

By spring training 1927, the conspicuous, full-page ads for Pennant Park, and most of the rest of Sarasota's developments, had disappeared. However, no mention of financial losses or editorials railing against McGraw for the failed development appeared in the press. In fact, an editorial in the *Sarasota Herald* lauded John J. and told readers, "The glad hand of Sarasota is extended in today's *Herald* to John J. McGraw and his stalwart band of swatters."

It is a safe bet that the failure of Pennant Park prompted McGraw to look elsewhere for a spring training site. When he was hit on the ankle by an errant ball during a training game in 1928, a misfortune that prevented him from traveling to Fort Myers with his team, it was noted by nationally syndicated columnist Westbrook Pegler:

> *There are those who say this blow to the ankle was something in the nature of a favor to Mr. McGraw, because a trip through Florida would have awakened unhappy memories of an expanse of jungle near Sarasota which Mr. McGraw and some associates were retailing to investors a few years ago at very interesting prices.*

The Giants had meant a lot to Sarasota. Floyd L. Bell, managing editor of the *Sarasota Herald*, told his readers:

> *Sarasota has been chosen by the most colorful team in America as its training grounds, because of the climate, the sunshine and the general atmosphere of the place...The selection of the city means also column after column of publicity* [in] *the great dailies of the metropolis* [that] *have their special representatives with the team.*

Of the players who came here he intoned:

> *There is no finer, cleaner, example of American manhood today than the average ball player. He is a gentleman, courteous, gracious and alert, keen minded and clear. It is a distinct pleasure to meet and to be associated with these fellows...It means that the city takes its place at once on the map as one of the most delightful sites in America.*

THE OTHER RITZ-CARLTON

Nothing so announces to the rarified world of first-class travelers that a city has achieved top-drawer status than the construction of a Ritz-Carlton Hotel.

Many trace Sarasota's most recent land boom and downtown resurgence to the Ritz-Carlton, which opened with grand fanfare at the end of November 2001 and went on to become one of the top-rated hotels in that chain of opulent hostelries.

The project, which was put together by former business associates and later courtroom adversaries Kevin Daves and C. Robert Buford, recalls a very similar scenario that played out in the local press nearly eighty years ago.

It occurred at the tail end of the Roaring Twenties boom and concerned a Sarasota Ritz-Carlton Hotel and two associates: businessman Owen Burns, the area's first major developer, and circus man John Ringling, art collector, railway man, banker and developer.

This duo had participated in many local projects together, driving Sarasota forward. As Ringling was away from Sarasota on business a great deal of the time, Burns became his point man, a hands-on supervisor who could be trusted to get the jobs finished. It was Burns's construction company that built the Ringling mansion Cà d'Zan and the first Ringling Causeway and purchased for Ringling much of the property that would make up his projects on Lido Key, Longboat Key and St. Armands Key. Burns's dredging company dredged and filled Golden Gate Point as the starting place for the Ringling Bridge; it also filled in much of the area around the various keys for which Ringling had such grandiose plans.

Burns also had his own major projects underway, and they were many: the Burns Court bungalows, Washington Park subdivision, the building at Herald Square, the Belle Haven Apartments, the Burns office building and the grand El Vernona Hotel, the most significant hotel in Sarasota up to that time and for many years thereafter.

Burns was also the vice-president and minor shareholder of Ringling Estates. Ringling was the president. Both men had high hopes for Sarasota, which had recently been discovered as a fashionable destination for wealthy snowbirds.

Initially, Ringling balked at the idea of constructing a hotel. At the beginning of the 1920s boom, Burns tried to convince him to garner concessions from the city and undertake a first-class hotel project downtown. Ringling demurred, and shortly thereafter, Andrew McAnsh constructed the Mira Mar Apartments and Hotel on Palm Avenue.

As the real estate market charged forward, Ringling's vision for St. Armands, Lido and Longboat as a winter nesting place for high-brow tourists crystallized. He determined that a Ritz-Carlton would ensure his success—it would draw a steady stream of affluent visitors to his keys.

Burns was already well into his El Vernona Hotel project when Ringling finally decided to move forward with the Ritz-Carlton. The timing for both gentlemen could not have been worse.

On Sunday morning, March 14, 1926, the *Sarasota Herald* headlined "Start Work on Ritz-Carlton Hotel Monday" and reported that it would be the greatest hostelry in the state of Florida and was expected to be completed "very soon."

Sarasota, it seemed, had truly arrived, but in fact the party was nearly over. Both Burns and Ringling were at the top of their games in the mid-1920s. The grand El Vernona, named for Burns's wife, was moving forward as scheduled, the Ringling Causeway was completed and thousands of people drove across to view St. Armands, Lido and Longboat Keys, with their wide, palm-lined streets, antique statuary and hallmark Harding Circle. Daily concerts were given by the Czechoslovakian National Band brought to town by Ringling to add excitement to the grand opening of the Ringling Causeway. Priced at $3,000 and up, sales of homesites on Ringling Estates, "America's Lido," were brisk.

But outward appearances belied the fact that by the beginning of 1926 real estate sales were slowing throughout Florida, and when the hurricane tore through Miami that September with such force and devastation, property values began to plummet and newcomers slowed to a trickle.

The Ritz-Carlton required $800,000 in capital, toward which Ringling put in $400,000 of his own fortune, and Ralph Caples was charged with raising the balance within the community.

As the five-story luxury hotel began to rise proudly on the south tip of Longboat Key, money began to dry up, progress slowed and only Ringling's funds kept the project moving forward.

It was at this juncture that Ringling began dipping into the assets of Ringling Estates, of which Burns held a 25 percent interest. Burns sought an injunction to prevent Ringling from "manipulating the Sarasota Ritz-Carlton Hotel Company and the John Ringling Estates, Inc. to require the one to stand for the obligation of the other." Burns saw his money being frittered away in an ill-advised attempt to fulfill Ringling's promise.

When Burns ceased to be vice-president of Ringling's company in 1927, there were nearly $4 million in assets and very little debt. Burns's suit claimed that Ringling was involved "in a studied scheme to cause John Ringling Estates to underwrite loans to the [Ritz-Carlton] hotel company" and ultimately confiscate Burns's 25 percent stake.

It would be difficult to find two men more different than Ringling and Burns. Burns was reticent, a gentleman and a loving husband and father. He shunned the spotlight, and his business dealings were aboveboard. Ringling, on the other hand, was boisterous and colorful—a showman. He had no children, and his marriage to Mable, whom he truly loved, was helped along, according to his nephew Henry North, by "Aunt Mable's loving acquiescence." Often his business dealings were convoluted and iffy—hiding assets when it suited him, exaggerating them when necessary.

Burns moved here in 1910 and bought out the holdings of the Florida Mortgage and Investment Company, and his business interests concerned only Sarasota. Ringling, traveling throughout the country with the circus, dabbled in numerous far-flung ventures: oil, ranchland, railroads, a stake in Madison Square Garden. He had homes in New York and New Jersey.

The two were never close. In letter and telegram exchanges, through which they conducted much of their business, it was always "Mr. Ringling" and "Mr. Burns," never "John" and "Owen." They did not socialize together.

The courtroom drama involving Ringling and Burns came to a head at the end of 1930. By then, Sarasota had suffered through the real estate bust and, along with the rest of the nation, was mired in the Great Depression. The optimism of the preceding decade was lost, and foreclosures replaced grand openings as the order of the day.

In the end, the duo reached an agreement, and Burns's charge of fraud against Ringling was dismissed. As set forth in the court's final decree: "Neither [of] the defendants, John Ringling, John Ringling Estates, Inc., or the Sarasota Ritz-Carlton Hotel company are guilty of any…fraudulent or illegal acts as charged in the bill of complaint."

It was a grave financial blow for Burns, who also suffered the loss of the El Vernona Hotel, which was sold at auction to the Prudence Company. To heap insult on injury, the Vernona would be purchased by John Ringling, who changed its name to the John Ringling Hotel. Interestingly, the John Ringling Towers were demolished, along with the Burns office building, by Robert Buford to make way for today's Ritz-Carlton.

Burns set up shop in the former *Sarasota Times* building across the street from the newly named John Ringling Hotel and began the Tre-Ripe Citrus Guava Preserving Company. He died at his home on August 27, 1937. He was sixty-eight. According to his daughter Lillian, he was not embittered by his experience with Ringling and just moved forward with his life.

Ringling's final years were painful and difficult. Mable died in 1929, he lost control of the circus, he was constantly feuding with family members and former friends, he entered into a marriage that quickly unraveled and embroiled him in an acrimonious divorce, he was hounded by creditors, he became gravely ill and he nearly lost Cà d'Zan, the sale of which was prevented only by his death a few days before it was to be put up at auction. Ringling died in New York on December 2, 1936. He was seventy years old.

As for Ringling's nearly completed Ritz-Carlton Hotel, it stood for decades as a forlorn reminder of the real estate crash and the breakup of a once productive business association. It was demolished by the Arvida Corporation in 1964.

LIDO BEACH PAVILION

The original Lido Beach Pavilion, on what was billed as "America's ideal bathing beach," was dedicated on September 2, 1926, before a crowd of over two thousand people. Said to be a natural step of John Ringling's interests in the beach improvement program, it was patterned in the "foreign style." The building, which cost $30,000, was financed by John Ringling, Sam Gumpertz and Owen Burns. For the occasion, the city declared a half holiday. Mayor Bacon called it a "beach of a holiday."

THE SARASOTA HIGH SCHOOL CREED, CLASS OF 1926

1. To accept willingly every responsibility, pleasant or unpleasant duty, that is for the good of the student body.
2. To do the very best in studies and athletics at all times.

3. To cultivate a spirit of fairness in all sports; to play the game for the game's sake, remembering that glory is not in never failing but in rising above every fall.
4. To be absolutely fair and square in the pursuit of my studies and to regard cheating as the greatest crime of all.
5. To obey all rules willingly, remembering that they are made by those who have our development and growth at heart.
6. To do everything possible to advance the standing and reputation of my school.

BREAKFAST AND A WINTER WHITE HOUSE

Breakfast for John Ringling, as described by his nephew Henry Ringling North in *The Circus Kings*, was conducted as follows:

Then the butler, Frank Tomlinson, entered carrying an enormous dish of fruit. Uncle John devastated it. I have seen him eat twelve king oranges and five grapefruits; or two pounds of Tokay grapes. Mangoes were the most fun. Nine was a fair average for him.

After the fruit he got down to the serious business of breakfast—a king-sized sirloin steak or a heaping dish of corned-beef hash with poached eggs all over it. Then the coffeecake and coffee.

After John Ringling became involved in the frenetic real estate boom of the 1920s, he effectively campaigned to publicize Sarasota, which, by extension, would enhance his own holdings here—what was good for Sarasota was good for John Ringling, and vice versa.

Everywhere the Ringling Bros. Circus toured, signs boasting of Sarasota's many virtues appeared on billboards and in circus programs. Ringling Isles was advertised in circus brochures as "The Most Beautiful Real Estate Development in the World...where the homebuilder will find the realization of his fondest dreams."

Ringling had helped persuade John J. McGraw to bring the New York Giants to Sarasota for spring training to garner publicity for Sarasota, which sports writers would send back to the major newspapers of the North.

One of Ringling's biggest coups was to have involved Warren G. Harding, the senator from Ohio who was elected the twenty-ninth president.

The 1920s

Ralph Caples, Ringling's friend, Sarasota booster and civic leader, had been in charge of Harding's train as the candidate whistle stopped across the country during the 1920 campaign. After Harding took office, Ringling hit upon the great notion of convincing him to use the Worcester mansion on Bird Key as the winter White House.

With that hope in mind, the streets on Ringling Estates were named to honor America's presidents, with Harding Circle the centerpiece of the grandiose project.

At the time, the only residence on Bird Key was the Worcester Mansion, built by Thomas Worcester of Cincinnati to be the retirement home of him and his wife, Davie.

Davie had discovered the small island in 1910 while in Sarasota recuperating from an illness. Described as "a woman of great heart [who] loved intensely all that was beautiful in nature and humanity," she had written to Thomas of the island's breathtaking beauty, ending with a hopeful, "This is what I want for my old age...Oh! Words cannot paint the scene, imagination cannot conceive of such grandeur."

Moved to please his wife, Worcester bought the fourteen-acre island from the state in 1911 and began fulfilling her wish. Sand from the bay bottom was dredged to increase the key's size, and Davie began designing her dream mansion, which she named New Edzell Castle in honor of her ancestral estate in Scotland.

The Worcester mansion took nearly three years to complete. Said to have cost $100,000 dollars, it was lavishly furnished and outfitted with such luxuries as electric lighting and acetylene gas. Looking at it from the shore, it "glowed with startling radiance." Sadly, Davie died before the New Edzell was completed, leaving a bereaved Thomas.

Ringling acquired the property in the early 1920s and offered the Worcester dream home to Harding shortly thereafter. According to Ringling, the president loved the idea and "displayed all the enthusiasm of a big boy over his contemplated vacation in Sarasota." Ringling noted that the president's desk was covered with pictures of the Ringling yacht *Zalophus*, which would be at his disposal during "his sojourn on it as a haven of rest."

Before the plan could be carried out, President Harding, beset by the scandalous dealings of some of his cabinet members, died unexpectedly in California, and with him went Ringling's winter White House coup.

THE AMERICAN BANK FAILS

Sarasota was well into the misery of the Florida real estate bust in May 1928 when the *Herald* announced that the American Bank on the southwest corner of Main Street and Palm Avenue was closed. There was no "run" on the bank, the paper assured readers. It was just a case of

the natural order of the business of the bank that it would be impossible for it to continue to do business and the directors took the only course open to them of calling in a national bank examiner and turning over the institution to him.

It was fully expected that depositors would be paid one hundred cents on the dollar and that "the failure is a natural one and is free of anything which savors of dishonor."

The building would become, briefly, the temporary home of the Palmer Bank until Palmer moved to its permanent location at Five Points.

In 1937, the building was transformed by Joseph A. Spadara into the Orange Blossom Hotel, a downtown favorite. Spadara, an Italian immigrant who arrived in America in 1900, was a rags-to-riches success story who developed in Sarasota, Fort Myers and Boca Grande, where he died in 1952 in the Boca Grande Hotel, which he had built in 1930.

JOHN AND MABLE

The true love of John Ringling's life was Mable. When she died in 1929 at the age of fifty-four, he was grief-stricken. His nephew, Henry North, wrote that Ringling was inconsolable at Mable's passing, giving away his brightly colored suits and ties and bemoaning that he would never be happy again.

Their twenty-five-year marriage had been characterized by an opulent and glamorous lifestyle, which included sumptuous homes, yachts, private railway cars, chauffeured automobiles, world travel, hi-brow acquaintances and art collecting on a grand scale. John Ringling was the circus king, and the beautiful Mable, "a striking brunette with soft brown eyes and black glossy hair," became his queen.

Both had come from humble backgrounds. He was the son of a small-town harness maker. Mable Burton was from a little-known farming area around Washington Court House, Ohio. By the time they met (it was either on the Boardwalk in Atlantic City or at a restaurant at the World's Fair in Chicago, depending on who is telling the story), he was well on the way to success in the circus world and in other far-flung enterprises: small rail lines, oil prospecting and real estate. Mable, who had been working in a shop in New Jersey or at a restaurant in Chicago, was a fast study and was brought quickly up to speed regarding the finer things of life and the social graces expected of the wealthy.

They began their marriage with a simple civil ceremony at the Hoboken city clerk's office on December 29, 1905. Within a few years, they discovered the relaxing charms of Sarasota, where they became closely involved in all aspects of the community—he with his development projects, banking and chamber of commerce duties; she by immersing herself in the social functions of the city, with luncheons, teas, bridge parties and evening soirées. The legendary parties she hosted at Cà d'Zan or onboard their yacht, *Zalophus*, were lavish affairs, sometimes attracting hundreds, with music often provided by the colorful Czechoslovakian National Band.

As John was arranging to bring the circus to Sarasota in 1927 to help bolster the faltering economy and advertise the community, Mable became a founding member and president of Sarasota's first garden club, the Founders Circle. Its intent was to beautify a Sarasota that was then showing the doldrums of the real estate bust. Mable was also active with the Woman's Club and helped raise money for various local charities.

Together, Mable and John worked closely with the architects on the plans for their palatial, Venetian-style home, Cà d'Zan (Mable even purchased a gondola in Venice and had it tied up at her bay-front dock), and also their namesake museum for which they had been collecting art treasures from throughout Europe.

When Mable died in New York, it was the beginning of a downward slide for John. After a period of mourning, cash-strapped from the real estate crash and facing the financial quagmire of the Great Depression, Ringling met, wooed and wedded Emily Haag Buck. She was more than a few years his junior, and whatever attracted them to each other quickly faded, leading to a contentious divorce.

A SOLITAIRE DEATH

It was noted on the front page of the January 26, 1927 edition of the *Sarasota Herald* that a thirty-year-old Miami Beach man, having become depressed that he lost at a game of solitaire, shot himself in the head and died.

THE COLSON HOTEL

Reminding its readers that some men achieve greatness in "writing, inventions or other lines of endeavor," the *Sarasota Herald* noted that E.O. Burns found his version of it in 1926, when he opened the Colson Hotel for "the colored population and colored tourists." Said to have cost him over $35,000, the twenty-eight-room hostelry offered a dance floor, a "sanitary" barbershop and a soft drink parlor. Four bathrooms and a clubroom were located on the second floor.

A ONE-LEGGED PARACHUTIST

When the Sarasota Airport was dedicated on January 28, 1927, in conjunction with the Sarasota County Fair, planes from around the state flew in to help with the celebration marked as the "Aeronautic and Children's Day at County Fair." The highlight of the affair was put on by "Peg" Malone from Detroit, "the only known one-legged parachute jumper in the United States," who set the audience aghast when he "leaped into space" and lived to tell the story.

OIL!

After it was obvious to only a few that the land boom had gone kaput, an executive committee, formed of some of Sarasota's foremost civic leaders, including J.H. Lord, met to determine whether oil might be found in Sarasota County. They reported as follows:

> *We, the committee…after mature deliberation and due consideration of all matters and things coming to our knowledge touching the probability,*

feasibility or possibility of finding oil in paying quantities in Sarasota county, we, your committee, are of the opinion that the chances for finding pay dirt are so great, the probability of reward is so large and the benefits to be derived by our community appear so munificent that we can but recommend to the citizenry of Sarasota county that a concentrated effort must be made in order to have a test well drilled in our county. It is the opinion of the committee based on a study of the geological and topographical conditions that it is highly possible that if and when a well is drilled to sufficient depth on proper location to be established by geological authorities that the same will be found to produce oil, committee further believes that the citizenry of Sarasota should be allowed to participate and assist in any drilling.

For the next few months thereafter, the possibility for oil was headline news in the paper, and a derrick was erected on a piece of land owned by John Ringling off today's Highway 41 near Englewood. Opportunities to buy in for a big payday were offered, and thousands journeyed to the spudding-in ceremony, which featured baseball great Rogers Hornsby, then in town for spring training with the mighty New York Giants.

But it was not to be. The only commodity that flowed forth was water, an abundance of which Sarasota already had.

RINGLING ART

Baron Von Hadeln, dubbed by the *Sarasota Herald* "the greatest living authority on Italian art," came to Sarasota in February 1927 to assess the artwork that John and Mable Ringling had collected. Impressed by what he saw, the baron prophesized:

Mr. and Mrs. Ringling are to be the means of making Sarasota the art center of the entire South and one of the leading art centers of the world. Gigantic as I knew Mr. Ringling's plans to be, ambitious as I knew him also to be, it was with a feeling of actual awe that I, on my visit here, came to a full realization of what the building of this Museum will mean to this section.

There is no exaggeration in my statement that it will mean bringing the Art Center of the South to Sarasota. Permit me to call your attention to the fact that at present after one leaves Washington, your beautiful capital city, there is in the South no great Art Gallery or Museum.

THE GREATEST SHOW ON EARTH

The Florida Land Boom was losing steam by the end of 1925 and is generally considered to have come to a near stop after the hurricane of 1926, which caused much destruction in Miami. Luckily for Sarasota, there were some projects in the works that proceeded onward, such as the county courthouse and Sarasota High School.

The obvious doldrums that the county was experiencing were temporarily mollified when John Ringling announced in 1927 that he was going to bring the winter headquarters of the Greatest Show on Earth to Sarasota from Bridgeport, Connecticut. Not only would it create jobs for Sarasotans, but the attraction would also become the most popular in Florida. Wherever the circus traveled, Sarasota would be advertised on billboards and circus programs.

The announcement was a banner headline in the *Sarasota Herald* over a picture of Ringling, with the caption that it was the most important step ever taken in this region.

Floyd L. Bell of the *Herald* wrote:

> *Sarasota's future, always bright, took on a more roseate hue yesterday than ever before and today whether or not the clouds overhang the skies, the sun will shine just a little brighter, the atmosphere a little clearer for every one in Sarasota...No show, no circus, no institution of its kind ever approaches in magnitude and splendor the Ringling shows.*

It opened to the public, appropriately, on Christmas Day 1927.

Sam Gumpertz, at the time a friend of Ringling and a top showman, promised that in March 1928 there would be a celebratory carnival and Mardi Gras that would be the greatest ever staged. "I will not confine my statement to saying that it will be the greatest in the United States," said Mr. Gumpertz. "It will be the greatest in the world."

The circus remained in Sarasota until 1960, when it moved to Venice, and throughout the world Sarasota was known as the Circus City.

FREE RIDES AND PRICE READJUSTMENT

Trying to bolster newspaper subscriptions after the real estate bust, the *Sarasota Herald* offered free aeroplane or motorboat rides to local boys and girls who brought in new subscribers. Two three-month subscriptions won a trip across the bay in Frank Giles's forty-mile-per-hour speedboat. For five three-month subscriptions, one received an exciting adventure aloft with a licensed pilot.

Trying to bolster sales on Longboat, St. Armands and Lido after the crash, Ringling announced a "readjustment" in prices for property there. In "An Interview With John Ringling" in the February 13, 1927 *Sarasota Herald*, he promised "to have a large portion [on Lido] set aside for the man of moderate means or salary who may purchase a lot and erect a home there."

THE REAL ESTATE BOOM (AND BUST)

A.B. Edwards, Sarasota's first real estate man, insurance man and mayor of the city of Sarasota, as well as the man considered to be Mr. Sarasota by generations of locals, summed up the 1920s real estate boom as follows:

I doubt if anything like that rush ever happened before or will ever happen again, particularly as it affected our City and County. It was worse than the mad rush to the ancient gold fields. The town filled up over night with land speculators and subdivision boys all dressed up in their loud plaid knee breaches and sailor hats, who rushed in and took over. Living and office accommodations were soon exhausted. Street corners were used for offices. Contracts and option blanks were carried in pockets. They were sleeping in cars, on street benches, and actually in the railroad waiting rooms. Buying and selling real estate options and contracts were running rampant. Sometimes options and contracts changed hands 4 or 5 times before the title would pass. Real estate prices began to jump skyward. Main street frontage went from $150 and $200 per front foot to $3,500; water frontage from $50 and $60 to $200 and $300...The City's population jumped from about 6,000 to 15,000 within a year's time. The high pressure boys were walking around with checks in their pockets for several days, too busy to deposit them in the banks. Then about the latter part of 1926 the high pressure boys were trading among themselves wondering what had happened; and by early 1927 the big real estate boom was all over. The water had been squeezed out of the sponge and the professional land traders and high pressure guys had moved out much faster than they *came in. And the permanent population of about 7,000 of us immediately set about to save what we could out of the wreck.*

Ordinarily it would have taken 100 years for the average American City to acquire the same amount of public and private improvements as did Sarasota during that two and a half year boom period.

THE 1930s

THE FUTURE OF SARASOTA

At the beginning of 1930, with the effects of the real estate crash well at hand and the Great Depression just underway, the *Sarasota Herald* promised the following to its demoralized readers in a January 27, 1930 editorial:

> *At the present time, Sarasota is in a state of adolescence. It is gawky and awkward and somewhat uncouth, but Sarasota has a future. It is inconceivable that a city situated as Sarasota is should cease to grow either in population or civic development.*
>
> *At the present time, Sarasota is but sparsely settled. The old city, which embraced about one square mile, is pretty well filled up with business houses and homes, but the outlying sections of the city, comprising the other 19 square miles, contain thousands of home sites which will gradually be utilized for building purposes and become the residences of thousands of citizens.*
>
> *There will undoubtedly come to our people, and to those who in the future come to make their homes with us, a birth of civic pride that will lead us all to renewed effort in improving our individual properties and in united civic endeavor, in beautifying our city... When we have outgrown our state of adolescence and come to the years of maturity, with all our natural advantages, we make bold to predict that Sarasota will rival, if it does not surpass, any city in the southland, in beauty and attractiveness. What Sarasota is to be may be a dream today, but tomorrow it will be a reality.*

THE RINGLING MUSEUM OF ART

Prior to the opening of the Ringling Museum of Art, the *Sarasota Herald* intoned in an editorial about what made Sarasota such a special community. It listed the farming potential, the circus winter headquarters and the John & Mable Ringling Museum of Art:

> *The art museum which will be open soon, as B.C. Forbes tells us, is something unparalleled anywhere in the United States in its excellence and attractiveness. Its magnificence is simply indescribable. As it becomes known and appreciated, it will prove a great magnet to draw people to Sarasota. Sarasota excels because it has more and greater attractions than any other city in south Florida. Delightful as it is to live anywhere in this section of the state, here the delight is supreme.*

THE WORLD'S RICHEST BOY

In 1933, Sarasota landed the Boston Red Sox for spring training, replacing the New York Giants, who did not return after the 1927 season. The new owner of the team was a young Thomas Austin Yawkey, who inherited $5 million and was told he was the world's richest boy.

According to a *New York Times* newspaper report, his mother put the amount of his wealth into perspective for him:

> *Mrs. Yawkey arranged a series of saucers on the table with varying heaps of beans, graded according to the wealth of the Rockefellers, Vanderbilts, Morgans and others, and in the last saucer she placed one bean to represent the Yawkey millions. This, according to the young man, was a comparison that he never forgot.*

THE LIDO CASINO

Trying to bolster flagging tourism during the Great Depression, Mayor Verman Kimbrough announced that there would be a quick start on a beach casino. The February 6, 1938 edition of the *Sarasota Herald* ran a pen and ink sketch of what was called SaraSands, offered by architect Albert Moore Saxe.

Kimbrough stated:

> *I am convinced that the great majority of the people of Sarasota are demanding that the city administration take immediate measures to start the construction of a municipal beach establishment that will be a credit to the resort pretensions of Sarasota.*

Pushed forward by the chamber of commerce Lido Casino Committee, construction on what was billed as the $100,000 casino was soon underway, but it was Ralph Twitchell, who would go on to be considered the grandfather of the Sarasota School of Architecture, who got the plum assignment.

Built on two acres at Coolidge Park on Lido Beach, the Art Deco plans called for two swimming pools, two dance floors, terrace restaurants and dining rooms and cabanas that arched on each side toward the Gulf of Mexico.

When it was completed, the *Herald* editorialized that Sarasota should be very happy:

> *This splendid structure…is the most beautiful beach casino on the west coast and perhaps in the whole state. From an architectural standpoint, it is a work of art. Standing prominently on one of the finest bathing beaches in the world, it challenges the admiration of everyone who sees it. This will mark an historic forward step in the development.*

Sarasota residents are still bitter—after forty years—that the Lido Casino was demolished. To paraphrase an old sports lament, "We wuz robbed."

Truly a spectacular sight, the building was as blindingly bright as the surrounding sand, accentuated with four towers and eight giant, concrete sea horses on the second floor, staring stoically into the distance; this was Sarasota's glorious beach oasis, a symbol of what life in a resort community was all about.

There was so much to do there: swim in the AAU-sized pool (an adjacent round wading pool served toddlers), dine and dance in the Casa Marina Room, grab a burger and Coke in the grill, enjoy a cocktail at the Castaways Bar, attend parties, card games and political rallies in the ballroom or just sit on the second-floor terrace near the sea horses and watch the passersby.

Such a building had never been seen in Sarasota, its modern style a far cry from the staid Spanish Mission and Mediterranean Revival look that had been the community's predominant architecture.

When World War II broke out and Sarasota became a training area for the Army Air Corps, this was one of the soldiers' favorite havens.

But nineteen short years after the fabled (and deteriorating) Lido Casino opened, the *News* editorialized in the November 6, 1959 edition:

What About Lido? Has the burial service been held for the two reports on Lido Casino? Just 64 days ago today, city commissioners found before them in a neat folder a detailed report on the ailing Lido from City Personnel Director William R. Montgomery.

Just 40 days ago today, a 91 page report on the same subject, with recommendations on how it could be remedied, was being written by Tec-Search Inc.—this one at a cost of $2,000 to the taxpayers.

Both reports left no doubts whatsoever that most needed for the sick and deteriorating beach resort was a good strong dose of good management.

But hardly a word has come from commissioners on either report.

The Tec-Search report calls for an aggressive promotional program to attract people to the casino.

But it's doubtful if you can do a very aggressive selling job on $100. Yes, that's what the casino advertising budget is for 1959–60.

That figures to about $8.33 a month for the next 12 months.

The commission must demand that the city manager act now to put Lido on the road back to its rightful place as a top attraction in our town.

In 1964, the issue of what to do with the casino was put to the voters. Would the citizens vote a bond issue of $250,000 to "remodel, modernize, and improve Lido Beach Casino…?"

The citizens voted yes. In April 1965, after engineers reported to the city commission that the Lido Casino's buildings were structurally sound, improvement work should have begun. But nothing happened.

On February 13, 1969, the Sommer's Wrecking Company began demolition. A few days later, the Lido Casino was a pile of concrete and twisted metal.

Just a month and a half earlier, on January 1, 1969, a picture of the casino, still in use, appeared on the front page of the *Sarasota Herald-Tribune* with the caption "Here visitors and residents flock to Lido Beach Casino." There was not a hint that it was about to be demolished. Consequently, there was no hue and cry from the citizens; no demonstrations or candlelight vigils protesting its destruction.

Former city mayor Jack Betz, who was on the city commission at the time and was the only commissioner who voted not to demolish it, said in a 1992 interview with me, "The people voted to remodel it. We didn't do that and I think it was wrong—I still think it was."

A Dollar a Snake

In order to rid Sarasota of the local rattlesnake menace, John R. Peacock, clerk of the court, offered a one-dollar bounty for each rattlesnake killed in Sarasota. It could be of any size, but in order to claim the dollar, the snake hunter had to swear that the snake was not caught in Manatee, Charlotte or some other county. And it was only necessary to bring a small portion of the snake, six or eight inches, and the rattlers. Payment was made in cash on the spot.

After the first week, it was announced that rattlesnake hunters were coming in daily, some with as many as fifteen to eighteen rattlers. One man refused to accept the dollar, asking that it be given to the Salvation Army drive instead.

Newspapers Merge

On June 12, 1938, David Lindsay, president of the *Sarasota Herald*, and Benton W. Powell, president of the *Sarasota Tribune*, announced that the newspapers were going to consolidate into the *Sarasota Herald-Tribune*. Their mutually signed letter printed on the front page of the *Sarasota Herald* noted:

> *There has been developing in Sarasota in recent months a fine get-together spirit. Today the city stands at the open door of great future advancement. Whether we enter that open door…depends in no small measure, on the willingness of our people to pull together in hearty cooperation to attain the worthy ends which appear to be within our reach.*

GOLF

Where was the game of golf in America first played? The controversy was taken up by the *Sarasota Herald* in the May 4, 1939 edition with a reprint from the *Atlanta Journal* written by O.B. Keller first published on November 15, 1931:

> *The semi-classic discussion of where golf was first played in America has popped up again. You'd never guess who started it this time.*
>
> *It was John Ringling, showman and art patron—none other.*
>
> *I was interviewing Mr. Ringling in Atlanta the other day, trying to learn about his $25,000,000 art museum at Sarasota, Fla.*
>
> *Mr. Ringling is one celebrity who does not like to talk about himself, which is refreshing and nearly unique, but not conspicuously helpful in finding out about a vast art collection. He was smoking a fine, strong black cigar and some way it reminded me of golf, perhaps because Walter Travis always used to smoke a cigar when playing.*
>
> *So I asked Mr. Ringling apropos of nothing, if he played golf.*
>
> *"I go through the motions," he said. "It's fine exercise, and say, did you know that golf was first played in America right down there at Sarasota? Fact! A colony of Scots settled there more than 50 years ago, and Colonel Gillespie laid out a course of four holes, later nine, and they had a regular club.*
>
> *"That was before the 'Apple Tree Gang' started their American St. Andrews club at Yonkers."*
>
> *I remember the latter. It is quite historical. Robert Lockhart and John Reid started that one in 1888.*

The full page of golfing news in that day's edition of the *Herald* also noted that a diary kept by Alex Browning stated that the great man had played on Gillespie's course in May 1886. Gillespie had asked him if he had ever played, and when Browning replied, "No," Gillespie said to him, "Mon, y're missin' half ye life."

Joe Williams, "noted sports columnist" of the *New York World-Telegram*, was quoted from an article he wrote on March 21, 1935:

> *The Yonkers adventure is, of course, completely authentic, but if any historian wishes to wager this club was the first to re-echo the piteous*

*cry of, "Boy, my niblick, please!" he should proceed with great caution
and frugality. To come right out and say so, he should keep his money
in his pocket.*

*Yonkers just wasn't the first golf club in America. The Sarasota Golf
club preceded Yonkers by at least two years. For some strange reason, this
interesting historical item has just been brought to light. There is indisputable
evidence that golf was played here in 1886. The widow of the man who
built the course is still alive to confirm the facts.*

*She is Mrs. J. Hamilton Gillespie, a gracious lady who lives here in
an attractive home. Her husband—very probably the father of American
golf—died on a golf course here 12 years ago. He came to this country
from Scotland along with scores of fellow adventurers, and soon the Merrie
Highlanders were hooking and slicing over a rough-hewn golf course.*

ROGER FLORY

Roger Flory came to Sarasota from Chicago in 1925, leaving behind a law
practice for a successful career in real estate. He recalled that shortly after
coming to town, he made $10,000 in two days.

As an example of that era's inflated prices, he cited a fifty-foot lot on
the corner of Washington Boulevard and Laurel Street that sold during the
1920s for $40,000 for use as a ten-story office building. It went for $600
in the 1930s as a site for a gas station. On North Palm Avenue, a property
bought for $50,000 by three local businessmen was sold in the 1930s for
$4,500. Bayside lots on Lido were offered at $5 a front foot and there were
no takers, nor were there buyers for Sarasota bonds offered at ten cents.
A $250,000 multistoried building constructed during the boom sold for
$35,000 plus back taxes.

Also a major civic leader and Sarasota booster, Flory, who was considered
Mr. Republican in Sarasota for his efforts to organize the Republican Party
into a strong force, was given a special gavel from the Sarasota County Board
of Realtors for his community service. The gavel was made of wood from
the homes of Washington and Jefferson, with a steel band from the "Mighty
Mo," the USS *Missouri*.

WHO IS BURIED IN RINGLING'S TOMB?

On December 2, 1936, Sarasota awoke to the news that John Ringling had passed away. The banner headline in that morning's *Sarasota Herald* told its readers that "John Ringling Dies in New York." Feature stories, along with Ringling's photograph, recounted "Mister John's" illustrious circus career, his varied interests outside the big top and even included an article recalling his "love for trees and flowers," intoning that the Australian pines he planted were his pets.

The flag atop the American Legion War Memorial in the center of Five Points was lowered to half staff, and so was the flag at the circus winter quarters. A wreath of flowers was laid on the steps of the Ringling Art Museum, and Mayor E.A. Smith sent a wreath to Ringling's New York residence.

Sarasota was in mourning. The great man had died.

No matter what people might have thought of the circus showman—his manner could be demanding, overbearing and gruff—few wished on him the angst of his later life. The slings and arrows that Ringling suffered during his last six years were almost endless.

His first wife, Mable, the love of his life with whom he shared the trappings of his triumphant rise in fortune, died in 1929, leaving him despondent.

His close friend Sam Gumpertz backstabbed him by helping to wrest away his control of the circus. He feuded with his nephews, John and Henry North, whom he came to distrust and whom he cut out of his will with a codicil that also reduced the estate of his only sister, their mother Ida, who had also fallen out of his favor.

He was never on good terms with his brother Charles's wife, Edith; their bickering was ongoing.

After control of the circus had been taken from him, Mister John was even persona non grata on the circus lot. The newspapers were heralding the widowed "Edith-Miss-Charlie" as "Woman Who Rules A Circus." Gumpertz was dubbed "Circus Boss." Ringling must have been galled.

His second marriage, to Emily Haag Buck, which began in 1930 when he was sixty-four, was an unmitigated disaster, ending in a drawn-out, acrimonious, tabloid-type divorce with juicy claims and counterclaims played up in the press throughout the country. He recalled his domestic hell as

just continuous nagging and scolding, finding fault with everything, cursing, screaming, quarreling…She always used the word son-of-a-

bitch [committed] *acts of extreme cruelty and habitual indulgence in violent and ungovernable temper...screaming at the top of her voice... flying into rages.*

Then there was Richard Fuchs. Ringling's personal secretary from 1919 to 1934, Fuchs turned on the circus man with a vengeance. In a four-page, single-spaced letter of resignation, he recounted their history and threatened to tell anyone who would listen, including the tax men of the federal government, where Ringling's business skeletons were buried. Fuchs said, "I expect to be very frank and open with the government." He allowed that he was tired of being taken for granted, working for no money and traveling to Sarasota at his own expense.

Thrown into the mix of misery was the fact that while John Ringling was a multimillionaire on paper—a man with Rolls Royces and a Pierce-Arrow; a man who had fêted the rich and famous of his day on his yacht, private railway car and bay-front mansion; a man who owned one of the finest collections of Baroque art in the world, housed in his own museum—was now cash-strapped and hounded by creditors. His nephew Henry wrote that at one time his uncle had over one hundred legal actions pending against him.

Ringling did not seem to have enough cash on hand to take a foursome to dinner. Toward the end of his life, his estate and furnishings were advertised in the legal section of the newspaper to be sold to satisfy his monetary obligations. The stress of his last year would have been enough to kill one of his elephants.

Lastly, and perhaps not surprisingly, he had been terribly ill. First he suffered a bad leg infection, then a thrombosis incapacitated him and later, when it was thought that he had regained his health, he caught a cold that turned into pneumonia and he died.

The circus king passed away in New York City, in his Park Avenue apartment. With him at the end were his lifelong friend Frank Hennessey, his physician Dr. Maurice Costello, his nurse Miss Saunders, his sister Ida and his nephew John North.

Perhaps the beleaguered Ringling took some bit of comfort from the thought that when he was laid to his much-needed rest, his desire to be buried with Mable in their crypt at their beloved museum would surely be carried out. Well, sorry, Mister John.

The rigmarole about his last few feet of earth should have been unnecessary. When the circus king turned art collector built the beautiful

John & Mable Ringling Museum of Art as a memorial for himself and Mable on property adjacent to Cà d'Zan on Sarasota Bay, he had his architect design a crypt in the courtyard opposite the entrance, under the imposing statue of David. Among the magnificent art treasures that he had collected over the years, he and Mable, the love of his life, would rest and be remembered forevermore by untold numbers of passersby. Or so he thought.

Ironically, the man whose life was spent wheeling and dealing, at keeping the circus wagons and then the circus trains on schedule throughout the length and breadth of America—it was said he had a genius for transportation details—could not get himself buried where he wished. In fact, he would not be permanently buried at all until nearly fifty-five years after he died.

The day after he died, the *New York Times* printed his biography, complete with his photograph, recounting his American success story as he rose from being a poor boy in a small town to one of the wealthiest men in America.

On December 3, the *Sarasota Herald* informed its readers of the funeral arrangements and burial plans under the headline "Bodies of Mr. and Mrs. Ringling Will Rest in Art Museum Crypt."

After a service in New York, his body was to be placed in the receiving vault at the Brookside Cemetery in Englewood, New Jersey (where Mable had been interred in 1929), and "at a later date (both) be brought to Sarasota and laid to rest in a crypt in the John & Mable Ringling Museum of Art." Exactly as he had wished it.

Time passed—a lot of time. Ida North and her sons, who had been told in a codicil to Ringling's will that

> *both my nephews, John Ringling North and Henry W. North for reasons good and sufficient to me, I have determined that neither of such nephews shall receive anything whatsoever in any form, shape or manner from my estate.*

Ida's inheritance was reduced to just $5,000 per year. But by the time the codicil was revealed, they had already taken over the muddled affairs of the circus and the Ringling Estates as executrix, executor and trustee, respectively.

No burial instructions were mentioned in the will, possibly because it was a well-known fact that Ringling had designed and built into the museum a crypt, and he may naturally have assumed that he would be interred there.

The 1930s

Certainly, there was no urgency in returning Uncle John and Aunt Mable to Sarasota and their crypt. It did not seem to be on anyone's A-list of things to do. As late as 1950, when Ida died, John and Mable Ringling were still being "temporarily interred."

John Ringling has never been out of Sarasota's consciousness. His name is everywhere to be seen here; his accomplishments for Sarasota are continually lauded. Thousands visit his mansion and museum annually, and his statue is prominent on St. Armands Circle. Add the Ringling School of Art and Design, the old RIngling telephone exchange and the Ringling Causeway and it's no wonder that the name Ringling is synonymous with Sarasota.

While the particulars of his death and his wishes for his burial have dimmed over the years, periodically the issue of his crypt and the whereabouts of his remains have surfaced.

In 1957, the *Sarasota Herald-Tribune* published an article by Lawrence Dame about the crypt and stated, "But a little-known dream to them—the burial of their bodies in a crypt at the open end of the museum's grand court, has never been realized."

At that time, the vault was being used for storage—so much for sentiment!

Dame quoted the museum's architect, John H. Philips, recalling in the mid-1920s that "Ringling talked much about a magnificent set of tombs where he and his wife would be placed for all time." He continued, "Ringling stopped, looked at the giant statue and suddenly declared, 'Philips, I want you to design the crypts and place them under the terrace, below the David.'"

The crypt was modeled after tombs seen in the Church of Santa Maria del Popolo in Rome.

In a follow-up story on September 10, 1958, Dame traced the movement of the Ringling bodies from an eighteen-year stay in a temporary vault in the Brookside Cemetery to a receiving vault in Hackensack, New Jersey, and then on to a crypt in Fairview Cemetery. At the end of the article, John Ringling was quoted from a previous Dame story as saying that he did not want to be buried in the Sarasota mausoleum "because I won't have people stamping on the terrace over my head." It was the first time any mention was made of Ringling not wanting to be buried in his memorial museum. It seems difficult to believe.

The odyssey of the remains of John and Mable did not end in Fairview, and soon his deceased sister Ida would join them in not being permanently buried.

Ringling wanted to be buried, along with his wife Mable, in a specially designed crypt beneath the statue of David in the courtyard of the John & Mable Ringling Museum. *Courtesy of the Sarasota County History Center.*

When Ida died in 1950, a small family service was held at her Bird Key home, where it was announced that her children planned to build a mausoleum for her remains. No one indicated where it would be placed or suggested that she might be buried next to her estranged brother John.

It was conjectured that she would be buried next to her husband, and in the meantime, she was interred at a Sarasota funeral home—for over forty years. The Ringlings seemed not to be into timely burials.

In 1960, trustees of the museum proposed that the bodies of John and Mable be brought to Sarasota and placed in a newly designed mausoleum. Chairman of the board of the museum George Higgins stated in a speech to the Downtown Kiwanis Club that the man who had given to the State of Florida property valued at least $120 million "should have his request for burial carried out."

More years passed by. Joe McKennon, longtime circus man and circus historian who was a contemporary of John Ringling, published a critical booklet, *Rape of An Estate*, and asked, "Why did John Ringling North as executor not bring them down and put them in their crypt? Why didn't the state, when it took it over in 1946, do something about this?" He went on, "It seems that removal to Sarasota was always blocked by relatives."

McKennon's booklet showed a rendering of the proposed mausoleum from the Ringling Museum; the likeness was presented to the state legislature, along with a request for $35,000 to finance its construction. Nothing came of it.

Jim Clark, Sarasota attorney and former board member and chairman of the board of the museum from 1972 to 1976, stated in an interview with me that during his tenure the board had looked at the possibility of returning the Ringlings back to the crypt under the statue of David, "as per their desire." Clark said that he and the board thought it would be a way to honor them for all that they had done for the community. He indicated that it did not happen because of interference from family members.

The bodies of John and Mable remained in New Jersey until 1987, when they were disinterred by Henry Ringling North, who had them moved to Restlawn Memorial Gardens in Port Charlotte, inching closer to Sarasota and possible interment at their museum.

North decided that he wanted his mother, Ida, buried with them on museum property. It would not be under the statue of David, and there would be no grand mausoleum. Museum trustees voted eight to one to allow his request. Other surviving relations fought to stop him. A court battle followed, pitting North against John Ringling's grandnieces, who wanted Uncle John and Aunt Mable buried in Baraboo, Wisconsin, and Ida buried next to her husband. Ultimately, Henry, then in his eighties and living in Switzerland, won out.

The trio ended up buried in a small and, putting it kindly, unpretentious plot on the museum grounds, as far away from their John & Mable Ringling Museum of Art as they could be and still be on Ringling property.

Sarasota Herald-Tribune writer Mark Zaloudek penned an article for the August 24, 1990 edition, quoting architect Matt Mathes, who described the design as "modest but fitting."

Henry was to pay the estimated $25,000 for the memorial. Larry Roggiero, the controversial head of the museum at the time, was quoted as calling the plan "terrific."

In November 1992, Henry paid a visit to the graves. Zaloudek quoted him as remarking, "That's the way I wanted it, because the house [Cà d'Zan] is there and it's quite a house. I think they'd be very happy, very pleased." Maybe.

John, Mable and Ida Ringling North are buried on the other side of this chain-link fence. *Author's collection.*

I went to the site on March 10, 2003. No markers pointed the way. I knew the approximate location from Zaloudek's articles. The grass needed mowing, wind-blown branches were scattered over the graves, the gates to it were locked with a rusting chain and the left gate handle was broken off.

A chain-link fence and shrubbery frame the area. Each of the three plots has a small bronze plaque inscribed with the name, date of birth, date of death and date of burial ("6/21/91"). I asked a lawn maintenance worker if the gates are ever opened. He didn't think so, but not to worry, he said, there was a space to squeeze through if I wanted to pay my respects. He offered that they were not buried where they wanted to be.

As I stared through the gate at the simple markers, it struck me that this was the antithesis of what the flamboyant showman stood for. The man who, more than any other, put Sarasota on the map and transformed it into the cultural haven that we brag about today, the man who gave the State of Florida a dramatically unique mansion and one of the finest museums in the country stocked with priceless works of art, has been repaid by being shunted away in a corner of his property near a toolshed, behind a black chain fence.

Stephen Lattmann, the architect and contractor who worked on the project, indicated that given the budgetary constraints, they tried to make the burial site as nice as possible. He thought that the location, given its proximity to the Ringling mansion, was appropriate. He, too, felt that considering all that Ringling had done for the community, "the man was short-changed."

The simple truth is that John and Mable, and even Ida, got a raw deal.

The Peculiar Death of Dr. Bergonier

The death of Dr. Eugene Bergonier was one of the most mysterious and colorful ever reported in the Sarasota press. The banner headline of the Monday, October 13, 1930 edition of the *Sarasota Herald* blared "Famed French Explorer Dies Here."

The obituary listed the cause of his demise as septic pneumonia. Funeral services were to be handled by the Thacker and Van Gilder funeral home, with the Reverend Father Elslander of St. Martha's Church presiding. This

Bergonier's strange death was headline news in the *Sarasota Herald. Courtesy of the Sarasota County History Center.*

was nothing out of the ordinary—a relative stranger in Sarasota's midst had passed on. Even Chief of Police S. Tilden Davis indicated an unwillingness to investigate "the unusual death" of the "rotund doctor."

The obituary noted that Dr. Bergonier's purpose in Sarasota was to "await the arrival of a tribe of 12 Ubangis, his long-lipped Africans with the Ringling show." Interesting, but, after all, this was the Circus City.

Dr. Bergonier had been the medical director on the Citroen Central African Expedition, which traveled fifteen thousand miles on half tracks from Algeria to Mozambique and Madagascar. The journey was documented in the June 1926 National Geographic article "Through the Deserts and Jungles of Africa by Motor" by George-Marie Haardt. It was on this expedition that Dr. Bergonier came in contact with the tribe whose women were noted for their elongated, pie-shaped lips—for them a sign of beauty.

Bergonier brought them out of Africa, first to tour Europe and South America and then, in 1929, to America, where they became a featured and very popular attraction with the Ringling Bros. and Barnum & Bailey Circus. Their disfigured lips created a sensation as they were paraded around the arena in front of the wide-eyed circus crowds. Part of the show included a lecture by Bergonier about their lifestyle back in Africa. The fact that some of the women had a difficult time keeping their blouses on did not detract from their popularity.

In Gene Plowden's book *Merle Evans—Maestro of the Circus*, the longtime circus band leader recalled that Ringling press agent Roland Butler gave the women their name and, in the ballyhoo of circus speak, advertised them as "the world's most weird living humans—New to the civilized world." On circus billboards they were billed as "Monster-mouthed Ubangi savages with mouths and lips large as full-grown crocodiles; from Africa's darkest depths!"

Before the end of the 1930 season's tour, Dr. Bergonier hastily left them in the care of Abdoulaye Samba, "his African Servant" of twenty-five years, and departed to Sarasota to await the tribe's arrival to the circus winter headquarters.

The king of the tribe, King Nebia, was not a man to trifle with. It was said that he could throw a two-pronged knife two hundred yards with accuracy and had bagged three hundred buffalo. He was also proficient with a boomerang. This prowess was well known to Bergonier, which explained his prudent departure to Sarasota.

The tribal leader believed that Bergonier had kept money that belonged to the tribe—money that was going to put the king and his people in good financial stead when they returned to Africa.

Ringmaster Fred Branda notes in his book *The Big Top* that Ringling paid the troupe $1,500 a week but that Bergonier only gave them a pittance and the tribe had to earn money selling picture postcards.

The bad blood between Samba, Bergonier and the traveling Ubangis, to whom the doctor referred as "my people," had been festering (Bergonier began carrying a revolver in his pocket) and boiled over in October, by which time they were all in Sarasota. Circus band leader Merle Evans said that the African troupe detested him.

The *Herald* reported that the Ubangis had become hostile toward Samba at the winter quarters and chased him from their tent. The trusty servant must have been past the two-hundred-yards mark before the king got to his knife or his boomerang, as Samba made it home alive.

There was also talk of hexes and black magic rituals involving pins and a doll that bore a harsh resemblance to Bergonier.

Indeed, by the tribe's way of thinking it was more the work of pins and needles and less a sandspur prick or an insect bite that felled the doctor. King Nebia was quoted by some circus folks as claiming, "No die, we make 'em die."

To be certain that, indeed, Bergonier had succumbed, either through insect bite or voodoo, Evans wrote that the king and three of his group went to the mortuary "and lifted up his eyelids to check."

Ringmaster Fred Branda recalled that the king (he called him Neard) and four of his wives "sprinkled powders and made scores of gestures to repel the doctor's evil spirit before they approached his body." Satisfied that he was deceased, they left.

The field day that the press was having with the colorful story angered Bergonier's wife; "excited her to a high pitch" is how the paper put it. She felt that the name and reputation of her illustrious husband had been tarnished. The widow wrote a comprehensive letter to the paper, which was printed in full, in French, with an English translation supplied by a French friend of the Bergoniers.

She demanded that the *Herald* immediately print a retraction using "big letters so that all his friends in Sarasota may know that my husband was honest, loyal and straight."

In part, Madame Bergonier wrote, "The articles which were printed in the *Herald* were false and defamatory and I demand excuses and if they are not made will ask my lawyer to sue them for defamation."

For its part, the *Herald*, through managing editor E.E. Naugle, indicated that the problem stemmed from a poor translation of what had been written:

The Herald *is sorry if Madam Bergonier has become offended through misinterpretation of the news stories and trusts that the publication of her note and this explanation will serve to disillusion her mind and ease to some extent the sorrow incident to the death of her husband.*

The apology was written in French as well so that Mrs. Bergonier could read it without interpretation.

A few days later, the paper also published a cablegram from George-Marie Haardt, who had led the African expedition of 1926:

Deeply affected, we send sincere condolences of all members of the expedition to the Dark Continent where Eugene Bergonier proved great qualities, big heart and brilliant intellect. We shall never forget such a faithful collaborator.

Madame was evidently appeased as no suit was filed. She made arrangements for her late husband to be taken back to the Bordeaux region of France for burial, and she bid farewell to the friends she had made in Sarasota.

On the same day that Mrs. Bergonier issued her complaint to the *Herald*, the Ubangi tribe set off for Africa. Three hundred citizens were on hand at the Seaboard Railway Station to get a final glimpse of the unusual-looking group.

John Ringling, who Branda said made a fortune off of them, bought their passage home.

The money they collected while touring with the circus was used to buy a ranch in Africa, "which they stocked with splendid cattle, and lived in high style among their grandchildren."

THE COMPLETE AND UNABRIDGED LEGEND
OF SARA DE SOTA

By George Chapline

One of the annual bright spots in Sarasota during the Great Depression (and beyond) was the annual Sara de Sota pageant, which drew tens of thousands

The 1930s

here to celebrate the legend of Sara, the daughter of Hernando de Soto, and her ill-fated romance with the Seminole Indian prince Chichi Okobee. Penned by George F. Chapline and first enacted in 1916, the legend goes:

Chichi-Okobee, the fleet and strong, heir by blood and physical prowess to the thousand tepees and stalwart warriors of Black Heron's Seminoles, stood motionless in the morning sun before the camp of the great white chief, De Soto. Two guardsmen with burnished helmets and shields and with naked blades drew nigh this prince of the Seminoles.

A harsh word of command broke the stillness of the sunbathed morning. With broad, brown palm uplifted—the sign of peace—and with steadfast gaze, Chichi-Okobee bade the guardsmen of De Soto draw nigh: "Peace, I surrender to the warriors of the great white chief." These were the words of Chichi Okobee. Bound, he was taken to De Soto. "Hold him hostage for our passage safe," said Hernando. Deep into the Everglades, skirting lakes and lagoons, parching upon blistering beaches, Chichi-Okobee was borne by the Spaniard. No murmur, no word of complaint escaped the captive's stoical yet princely lips. He had beheld Sara, the lovely daughter of the white chieftain; Sara, lovelier than all the princess maidens of the Seminole camp. He had surrendered himself a willing captive that he might suffer the throngs of captivity, the humiliation of bonds, that he might occasionally feast his own lustrous eyes upon the orbs of this princess of the house of De Soto.

But Chichi fell ill. The confinement, the lack of the food of his fathers, the want of his body for the long stride of the chase, the absence of the medicine man, and most of all the unsatisfied heart yearning, had done their work, and Chichi lay helpless, wasting, parching, dying of the fever of the Everglades.

Their efforts in vain, the physicians of the Spanish camp gave up. The Seminole prince must die. Sara De Soto begged permission to minister in the dying hour of Chichi-Okobee. Her ministrations wrought a marvel. Chichi mended. Love's potion more powerful than the medicaments of medicine men, brought back the steady gaze to the eye, brought back health and strength to Chichi.

Now was the daughter of De Soto taken ill. The physicians of the camp hung over her tapestried couch with the tender solicitude of fathers, yet all in vain; the malady that had stricken her seemed all the stronger for their care. Chichi begged of De Soto that he might go to his father's camp and fetch the great medicine man, Ahti—the medicine man who knew the secrets of the bad spirits of the Everglades. Though a man might be dead, yet it had been known that Ahti's skill had brought back the throb of the hearts.

111

Chichi-Okobee had tired the small deer of the forest, and his long, lithe limbs had won him many trophies in the sports of his tribe, yet never sped he so fast; never had the tropic trees beheld such speed as this bronze young prince plunged by them. One moon and yet another and Chichi-Okobee, with Ahti, the medicine man, stood before the tent of Sara De Soto. Strange incantations were uttered, mysterious herbs were offered in more mysterious smoke, that the spirit of the swamp might be appeased. Long vigils did Ahti keep by the side of the dying girl. Chichi stood mute with out the camp, with his eyes fixed upon the idly flapping doorway of the sick girl's tent. A black heron screamed and plunged over Chichi's head into the gloom of the forest. The great medicine man came forth from the tent, rending his deerskin cape. Chichi read the message—Sara was dead. The Great Spirit had called her. Ahti's powers had been matched with one greater than his.

Chichi sought the presence of De Soto and there poured forth to the Spaniard the love he bore for the dead girl. He begged that he might select the place of her burial and take part in the ceremony. De Soto, struck with the earnestness of the young Seminole, and melting under the caressing melody of his rich voice and savage eloquence, gave consent.

Okobee told of a land-locked, peaceful bay, the loveliest spot along the gulf-kissed shores of Florida, as the spot where he wished to bury the matchless Sara. He begged for and received permission to go to his camp and secure a body of his fellow warriors to make up a guard of honor to attend upon the last rites of his dead sweetheart.

On the morning following his departure, there appeared, drawing nigh De Soto's camp, winding in silent, single file, a body of 100 Seminole braves, at whose head came, Chichi-Okobee. All were bedecked in full war paint, all bore the solemn mien of their young chieftain; every quiver bristled with its complement of stone-tipped arrows; every bow was strung. Chichi-Okobee's war bonnet swept the earth; as he walked, his jasper-tipped spear flashed in the sunbeams, and like his followers, his quiver was filled with the arrows of warfare.

Three large canoes, bedecked with dark mosses of the forest, swept up the beach, propelled by the swift, strong strokes of six solemn Indians. In the first and largest of these the body of Sara De Soto was tenderly laid, De Soto and one guardsman were the sole passengers aboard this death craft, save Chichi-Okobee and six stalwart Seminoles who propelled the canoe. Silently the hundred braves took their places in the two remaining canoes. Silently, the leading canoe swept out and up the bay followed by the other two. At midday, Chichi-Okobee bade the funeral fleet come to a stand. In the middle ground of the most peaceful, the most beautiful body of water that the Spaniard had ever beheld, Okobee would bury his love. With the white bay flowers in her blue-black hair, and the feather from the wing of the black heron in her hand, the remains of Sara De Soto were lowered into the deep. Chichi-Okobee was rowed to the leading canoe of his followers, where he mounted the prow, leaving Hernando, his guardsman and oarsmen in the funeral barge.

Behold! A wonderful thing transpired. At a signal from the young chief every warrior sprang to his feet, tomahawk in hand. In strange, weird unison the war chant of these hundred warriors lifted itself and swelled across the bosom of the bay.

As its mystery-laden echo died away in the deep of the forest along the shore line, the blades of 100 tomahawks crashed into the frail bodies of the two war canoes. A moment of ripple, a moment of bubbles, and all was still. De Soto and his companions, in silent astonishment, gazed upon the grave of Chichi-Okobee and his hundred companions-at-arms—they had gone to guard the resting place of their chieftain's love.

The bay—"Sarasota Bay," as it has since been known—like a mirror of steel, reflects the doings of the stars and whispers to the caressing winds the story of the love of Chichi-Okobee and the beautiful Spaniard.

The elders of the Seminoles repeat the legend of the children, and say that the spirits of Chichi-Okobee and his warriors are in eternal combat with the spirits of evil and the children of the storm god, holding the pass to the gulf and protecting the resting place of Sara De Soto.

It is said in the sullen roar of the gulf, as it breaks upon the beaches, is but the noise of conflict, and that the whitecaps which chase each other and break and tumble across the pass are but the wraiths of the warriors of Okobee and the children of the sea, tossing their spirit arms, and meeting in never ending contest for the possession of the bay.

This, the legend of the lovely Sara and Chichi, the fleet and strong—the legend of Sarasota bay.

It is peaceful, it is beautiful.

George Chapline died before his legend became the popular mainstay of the Sara de Sota pageant. He passed away in 1913 at only forty-one years of age. He was remembered in the *Sarasota Times* as

a charming man highly gifted in every respect. Besides his being a preacher, a lawyer and legislator, in each of which positions he exhibited remarkable ability, he was also a widely read scholar, a captivating orator, a brilliant writer, and a great lover of music, in which last capacity he also excelled as a vocalist.

MISTER JOHN'S D-I-V-O-R-C-E

It may not have been much of a marriage, but it sure was a swell divorce.

John Ringling, "Circus Czar," took the matrimonial hand of Emily Haag Buck, a youngish divorcée, in a civil ceremony in the office of his friend Mayor Frank "Boss" Hague of Jersey City on the evening of December 19, 1930. His best man was Thomas McCarter, president of the Public Service Coordinated Transport of New Jersey. Emily's sister, Mrs. Howard Bradley, served as maid of honor. A few friends attended.

The marriage lasted a contentious three years and four days.

Their lengthy divorce, christened by some of the nation's papers "A 3-Ring Lawsuit," took on a life of its own and continued for years. One tabloid account of the Ringlings' free-for-all marriage printed in *American Weekly, Inc.* termed their life together "Mr. Ringling's Own 3-Ring Domestic Circus" and pegged Emily as "something between a steam calliope and a tigress at large."

John met the tigress on the Fourth of July 1930 while each was vacationing in Amsterdam. She was a bobbed-haired, blond beauty with bright, happy eyes and a sweet smile. She claimed to be thirty-four years old, stood a willowy five feet, five inches tall, weighed 110 pounds (give or take), liked cocktail parties and dancing and had an enviable bank account, no mean feat in 1930. She was one of the swells, always dressed to the nines and up for a good time.

John Ringling was a big man with a larger-than-life personality and a universally known name popularized by the Ringling Bros. Circus. His acquaintances were important personages in politics, business, entertainment and sports. He was once considered one of the wealthiest men in America. At the time of their meeting, he was a widower—he told her he was fifty-two but was really sixty-four—whose better years were behind him and whose future was looking bleak.

Although they saw each other only a few times in Amsterdam, Ringling began to woo the starry-eyed Emily through cablegrams and telephone calls. Upon her return home to her apartment in the Barclay Hotel in New York City at the end of September, he came to call on the evening of her arrival. Love was in the air—or at least something like it.

John Ringling and his then friend Sam Gumpertz (far right) are dressed in Spanish costume for the popular 1928 Sara de Sota celebration. Standing between them is Miss Frances Edwards, who was crowned Miss Sarasota that year. She was the daughter of A.B. Edwards, the city of Sarasota's first mayor. *Courtesy of the Sarasota County History Center.*

The day after the nuptials, the couple left by train for Sarasota, the town John helped to build, brand and put on the map. The *Sarasota Herald* ran Emily's photo, a caption about the marriage and, in another story, noted that Mrs. Charles Ringling held a reception in their honor. The paper called it the most brilliant party of the season, complete with an orchestra that played into the night, and it was attended by the who's who of local society.

That gay evening would not be a preview of their life together.

John's first wife and soul mate, Mable, with whom he shared his best and most productive years, died in 1929 of Addison's disease, and he had only recently managed to recover from the loss. He was also reeling from a series of financial setbacks caused by the Florida real estate crash, the Depression of 1929 and, later, a dubious decision to buy out his circus competition. He was heavily mortgaged, and his financial woes would only become worse. So would his health.

But when John and Emily met, he still enjoyed the impressive accoutrements of a wealthy man—a sumptuous private railway car, a luxurious mansion on Sarasota Bay, a Park Avenue apartment, Rolls Royces and a fabulous art collection housed in his personal museum—and he headed the largest and most popular circus in the world. Ringling was also into oil, real estate development and railroads, but alas, though filthy rich on paper, he was cash-strapped. Emily did not own a railway car, a Rolls Royce or a luxurious bay-front mansion, but she had a hefty amount of money.

Whatever else big John saw in bright-eyed Emily, her money had to have been near the top of the list. Four days before the couple became man and wife, John borrowed $50,000 from her and promised to pay it back in three months. On the afternoon of their wedding, he asked her to meet him at his apartment and proffered a document for her to sign away her dower rights. He said she signed on the dotted line and tore it up later; she said she tore it up but had never signed it.

"He said, she said" would be the theme of their divorce.

Whatever her motives in marrying the financially besieged gent who was old enough to be her father, she did express her love for him. In a long and longing letter mailed two days before Valentine's Day 1934, she began "Dearest One" and went on:

> *I wish I was with you darling. Dearest, don't worry about a thing, take it easy. Let your lawyer worry, get well, come up to me. I need you so, I long so for you Oh dearest you can't imagine how lonesome I am for you sweet dear. I love you. I love you until my dying day.*

She ended with "Your devoted & loving wife, Emily."

Her profession of love notwithstanding, matrimonial strife was right around the corner.

The sweet tone of her letter was the polar opposite of Ringling's characterization of Emily as an ever-argumentative, name-calling, contentious, inconsiderate, cold-hearted, meddling, money-grubbing hellion whom he had to divorce before her behavior killed him.

Ringling was represented by Henry L. Williford and James Kirk.

> *Question to John Ringling regarding an alleged assault on him by Emily:*
> *Did she hit you a pretty hard blow?*
> *Answer: Very hard for a woman.*
> *Question: It didn't hurt you in any way, did it?*

John Ringling's yacht, *Zalophus*, docked in Sarasota Bay across from the Sunset Apartments, which had been built as the Sarasota Yacht and Automobile Club. *Courtesy of the Sarasota County History Center.*

This photograph of the Sarasota County Bar 1935 shows both of Ringling's attorneys, James Kirk and Henry Williford, during the acrimonious divorce. *Courtesy of the Sarasota County History Center.*

Answer: It felt like [Primo] *Carnera for a minute or* [Joe] *Louis—it hurt, yes.*

Ringling filed his first divorce suit against Emily in July 1933, and it took her by complete surprise. She was served papers while shopping on Main Street in downtown Sarasota. As she recounted the embarrassing incident:

> *I went into one of the stores and while I was in there buying something, this process server came up to me and said, "Are you Mrs. John Ringling?" And I said, "Yes." And he said, "I have a summons for you." And I said, "For me?" and he said, "Yes, Mrs. John Ringling." And I said, "Why who could be serving me?" And he said, "I believe it is from your husband." And I said, "My husband? There must be some mistake. You must mean Mrs. Charles Ringling."*

In court, Emily stressed that there had been no talk of divorce in the Ringling household. "It was a complete shock to me."

Immediately after she had been blindsided by the server, Mister John and his private duty nurse, the ever-present Miss Ina Sanders, drove up. Emily testified that she asked him, "John, what is all this? I don't understand this at all." She told the court that he just laughed about it and did not say anything. "When I would say something he would just laugh. It seems I must have fainted because the next thing I remember, I was up in my bedroom."

The incident occurred two days after Emily said she caught the thirty-one-year-old Miss Sanders, described in one newspaper as "comely but plump," in pajamas sitting on the arm of Ringling's chair. The two were embracing. Emily's version of that night went as follows:

> *I noticed Miss Sanders there walking around in pajamas and in fact she had been sitting on the arm of a* [bedroom] *chair embracing Mr. Ringling. When I opened the door and walked in she jumped up from the chair. I said, "Miss Sanders, the best thing for you to do is leave in the morning. I don't need your services any longer."*

Seemingly nonplussed, Ringling told her, "Emily let's forget this now and in the morning we'll talk it over."

The 1930s

In later testimony about the alleged indiscretion, Ringling was asked:

Did Miss Sanders ever embrace you?
Answer: Never.
Question: What was your relationship with her and her relationship with you?
Answer: Simply I was patient and she was nurse.
Question to Nurse Sanders: Did Mrs. Ringing come into the bedroom of Mister Ringling and find you in pajamas sitting on the arm of the chair Mister Ringling occupied?
Answer: Certainly not.

Besides, the judge was told, Ringling's bedroom chair is a yellow Empire chair and has no arms.

Both John and Nurse Sanders stated that the first time they heard this spurious allegation was in the courtroom. Ina slept in John's bedroom on one of the twin beds, she said, at the behest of Dr. Joseph Halton. Emily contradicted this by saying that it was John's idea to have his nurse as a roommate.

The day after the service of the first set of divorce papers, Ringling discovered a distraught Emily with her sister packing her bags. After inquiring what she was doing, he beseeched her to remain at Cà d'Zan, his sumptuous Sarasota bay-front mansion. "Don't be so foolish, why don't you just stay here?"

Stay she did throughout the month of August, during which time "he hounded her" about extending the $50,000 loan and signing away her dower rights to the John & Mable Ringling Museum. If she would do that, he would withdraw the divorce.

He testified that it was she who begged to stay. In either case, Emily relented and signed the documents on August 31, 1933, agreeing to extend the $50,000 note for four years and receive interest of 6 percent. As security, five paintings were listed on the agreement as assigned to Emily: "Oil painting of General Benvenutti, by Moroni; Portrait of Queen of Cypress, by Titian; St. John, by Rembrandt; Portrait of a Lady by Rembrandt; Portrait of Olicano, by Franz Hals."

Nurse Sanders remained, and John had the divorce complaint withdrawn the next day.

John Ringling was a man whose habits included drinking twelve-year-old Scotch whiskey (Emily said he had several hundred thousand dollars worth of pre-Prohibition hooch under lock and key and protected by the Holmes Protective Agency), smoking good cigars, dining well and getting his own way.

He threatened her, she said, that in a Florida divorce court he would certainly prevail. Emily testified that the pressure he put on her to sign an extension to the loan and also sign away her dower rights was formidable—a civics lesson in the World According to John Ringing.

The Sunshine State in general, and Sarasota, the Circus City, in particular, owed him, Ringling told her. And public sentiment, "on account of his benefactions and contributions to the community, was strongly in his favor." He boasted to her that what the State of Florida had done for Henry Flagler—amending a divorce law in Flagler's favor—could be accomplished for him with little difficulty.

Finally, and perhaps most importantly to the socially conscious Emily, she said he assured her that "the wife from whom a divorce was procured on the grounds of cruel and inhuman conduct and violent and ungovernable temper…would be completely disgraced."

She was, she told the court, "frightened and coerced," worried that she "would be ruined with all my friends."

Ringling had a different story to tell. Emily had finally recognized the evil of her ways and promised to change, to do everything in her power to make his life a happy one, and swore that she would never again argue or contend with him over business matters. "She was on her knees to me every day, sometimes 3 or 4 times a day," he said, "begging me to withdraw the suit, offering to give me money."

> *Question to Mr. Ringling: Was it the execution by Mrs. Ringling of these documents* [the extension of the bank note and the release of her dower] *or was it because of her promises not to annoy you but to help you to be restored to your health and her promise to be a dutiful wife?*
>
> *Answer: No amount of money would have prompted me to live with her again and take that abuse.*

Ringling allowed that his life had become tolerable again. "The conduct of the defendant did in fact improve," he said, "and she desisted from her acts of extreme cruelty and habitual indulgence in violent and ungovernable temper."

The reconciliation was short-lived, however, and for whatever reason, Mister John would have his divorce. And it would be, to use a word popular at the time, a doozy.

THE 1940s

TIME CAPSULE

Sealed in a copper tube and placed in the cornerstone of the newly built Chidsey Library was the May 11, 1941 edition of the *Sarasota Herald-Tribune*. America had not yet entered World War II, which had been raging in Europe since September 1939.

The front-page story about the time capsule, along with a photo of the library, was beneath the banner headline "Six-Hour Nazi Raid Leaves Whole London Blocks Afire."

Both the world and local news had been bleak for quite some time, and the *Herald*'s editorial noted:

> *This edition of the* Sarasota Herald-Tribune *will be deposited in a copper tube in the corner stone of the John T. Chidsey library building this afternoon. We have no idea as to the time when this tube will be opened and this newspaper read by a future generation. It may be in twenty, or fifty, or one hundred years. It may never be read, if, at some future day, a blitzkrieg of bombers devastates Sarasota as are many towns in Europe being devastated, in this year 1941, in the savage war now being waged by ruthless men seeking domination of the world…*
>
> *However, if and when the tube is opened, we want the Sarasota citizens of that day to know that the people of Sarasota of 1941 were a happy and contented and forward looking folk, always striving for the up building and betterment of their city and deeply concerned for its welfare. Those of us who in the earlier days of the city, laid its foundation and contributed to its*

up building, have always cherished the hope that, in future years, those who were to come after us would find our work well done and our faith in the city's future development fully justified in the comfort and happiness which its citizens of distant days will enjoy.

In behalf of the present day citizens of Sarasota, we extend to the citizens of the Sarasota of future years the most cordial greetings. We hope they will find an even greater joy and more extended benefits in living here than have fallen to our lot. There will still be here the beautiful beaches, the broad expanse of the bay, the marvelous climate, the luxuriant vegetation, the matchless sunsets, for their enjoyment, and, we trust, much more that will come into their lives through the future contributions of science and art to minister to their comfort and entertainment. We cherish the hope they will remember us gratefully for what we have done to prepare for them a place in which they may live and work and play under conditions favorable to a happy and contented life.

BLACKOUTS AND FLAG-RAISING

On January 2, 1942, Sarasota practiced its first total blackout, transforming itself "from a gay white way of peace into the shrouded blackness of a business like rehearsal for war." Throughout the war, blackout practices were held, and on Lido Beach, neon lighting was banned to prevent silhouetting navy ships in the gulf.

A few days later, in a show of Allied support, a formal flag-raising ceremony was held at the entrance to city hall, which was located in the Hover Arcade at the foot of lower Main Street. Along Gulf Stream Avenue, between city hall and Cedar Point Road, nine flags were raised representing the United States, the Red Cross, the British Empire, Soviet Russia, the Republic of China, the Dominion of Canada, the Australian Commonwealth, the Republic of Cuba and the Kingdom of Greece. More flags were to be raised representing all the nations that were fighting the Axis powers.

Mayor E.A. Smith intoned:

This is more than a flag-raising; it is dedicating ourselves to the cause of our allies. This is the time for us to dedicate ourselves to pulling together...It is a lovely country, it's a splendid world, but it's only as good as we make it.

Main Street, looking west from Orange Avenue, circa 1940. As today, parking was at a premium, especially during the bustling tourist season. *Pete Esthus Collection. Courtesy of the Sarasota County History Center.*

GARGANTUA THE GREAT

Four years after the fictional gorilla King Kong was shot off the Empire State Building by swooshing biplanes in the 1933 RKO movie of the same name, Gargantua the Great was brought discretely to Sarasota aboard the *Orange Blossom Special* and taken out to the winter headquarters of the Ringling Bros. and Barnum & Bailey Circus.

If there's no business like show business, so too, there is no hype like circus hype, and the press agents immediately set about the colorful task of transforming a lowlands gorilla, by way of Brooklyn, into "the most fiendishly ferocious brute that breathes," "the mightiest monster ever captured by man," "the world's most terrifying living creature." Take your pick.

Scoring Gargantua was a major coup for the North brothers. John Ringling, the last of the original circus men, had died in 1936, and Henry Ringling North and John Ringling North, his nephews and co-executors of his estate, found themselves in the center ring, running the show. Their purchase of Gargantua would play a major role in the circus fortunes, while establishing that John and Henry were true showmen, the chief requisite to successfully running the Greatest Show on Earth.

They had heard about the animal when they were in New York through a phone call from its owner, Mrs. Gertrude Lintz, who lived in Brooklyn and who had purchased the disfigured creature from a ship's captain. It seemed that in those days the buying of exotic animals was on the same plane as buying a used Packard—no big deal if you had the money. When asked once how much he paid, John reportedly said, "He's worth $100,000." Someone else put the number at $10,000—that's Depression-era dollars—and the admissions paid to see Gargantua helped the circus limp through the rest of the Great Depression.

Mrs. Lintz bought him as an infant, named him Buddy and treated him as one of the family, doting over him, letting him romp around her house and even having him present for her afternoon tea. But the sobriquet "Buddy" did not convey that this was "the world's most terrifying living creature," and besides, Buddy was the nickname of Henry North. It was he, trained in the classics at Yale, who renamed the animal after the giant in François Rabelais' book *Gargantua and Pantagruel*.

Of course, Buddy's true lineage did not make it into the circus programs, nor did the fact that he liked to pitch a softball back and forth through the bars of his cage or play tug of war with four or five men on the other end of the rope. As Henry North recalled in his book *The Circus Kings*, "He was a wonderful animal."

By the time Buddy was eight, he was becoming too much for Mrs. Lintz to handle. It was reported that during a late-night thunderstorm, a frightened Buddy awoke and startled her in her bedroom. One account had it that he had actually gotten into her bed. By this time he was well over three hundred pounds of pure power. Mrs. Lintz feared that he would escape into the neighborhood and perhaps forage for a Fay Wray look-alike, a fear that prompted her to call the Norths.

Several features of Gargantua needed no embellishment. His scowl was truly frightening. He was huge, and when he became angry he could be terrifying. Worldwide publicity was pumped up by circus press agent extraordinaire Roland Butler. Colorful billboards portrayed Gargantua the Great holding aloft a frightened-to-death African native in one hand. Another, showed a riled-up Gargantua, larger than life, with his arms raised menacingly, with the caption, "The Largest And Fiercest Gorilla Ever Brought Before the Eyes of Civilized Man."

When Gargantua bit John North (a testament to his fierceness), press releases immediately hit the news wires everywhere. *Life* magazine featured him, as did the *Saturday Evening Post*, the *New Yorker*, *Collier's*, the *American Weekly* and even the *Ladies' Home Journal*. Former heavyweight champion Gene Tunney wrote an article about how he would take on the hairy hulk in the ring. Tunney was certain he could knock him out—Dempsey must have hit him harder than we thought!

Gargantua was suddenly a star, his name a household word. As gorillas are susceptible to colds and pneumonia, the circus contacted the Carrier Air Conditioning Company to build him what would be termed a "jungle-conditioned cage," which replicated the climate of the Congo. It was a rolling cage, over twenty-six feet long, lined with thick glass panels outside of the bars. The temperature was kept at seventy-six degrees and the humidity at 50 percent.

According to North's book, Gargantua grew to five feet, seven inches and weighed 550 pounds, with an outstretched arm span of over nine feet and fingers the size of large cigars.

What the big ape needed was a companion—preferably a female—with whom to pass the time when the lights dimmed and the flaps went down on his "jungle cage."

Enter M'ToTo, which was said to mean "Little One" in Swahili. No Fay Wray to be sure, but great or not, Gargantua didn't get out enough to be picky.

M'ToTo was smaller than her soon-to-be hubby and had a "sweet disposition." John bought her in Cuba from Mrs. Stephen Hoyt, another lady who liked to sip her tea in the company of a gorilla. Go figure.

Once again the circus press agents sprang into action. In 1941, a wedding was arranged at the winter quarters, with Mrs. Hoyt "dressed in flowing chiffon and a picture hat" acting as the matron of honor, and as many press men as possible were rounded up to witness and report on the nuptials. There were flowers galore, a wedding cake was flown in from Schrafft's Bakery in New York and, as the moment approached, Lohengrin's "Processional" was played. M'ToTo's cage was painted white and bore the sign "Mrs. Gargantua the Great."

The happy couple's cages were backed up to each other, and when the backboard to M'ToTo's cage was removed so that the ceremony could begin, Gargantua, according to North, "stopped dead in his tracks. An expression of dawning amazement grew on his terrible countenance...he was plainly thunderstruck."

Thunderstruck or not, the next scene wasn't pretty as bride and groom ended up in wedding rage, throwing vegetables and grabbing ferociously at their cage bars. (Today this is the stuff of reality TV.)

The couple would never, much to the chagrin of circus management, consummate their marriage. Mrs. Gargantua, as she was thereafter known, tried to warm up to the big lug, but he wasn't having any part of it and kept his distance. Undaunted, the ever-resourceful circus management "adopted" two baby gorilla's for them, Gargantua II and his "foster sister" Mlle. Toto, and featured them as a family in the circus program, noting, "The cage which once bristled like a Sing Sing cell-block with the sullen menace of Gargantua and the unfulfilled M'ToTo is now warm and friendly." Right.

Gargantua the Great died in Miami in 1949 after the last stand of the circus season. His remains were donated by Henry to the Peabody Museum of Natural History at Yale, Henry's alma mater.

Mrs. Gargantua, doomed to go through life unrequited, became the namesake for John Ringling North's M'ToTo Room lounge, a wildly popular

The popular M'ToTo Room lounge in the John Ringling Hotel featured dancing to the orchestra of Rudy Bundy. When John Ringling North opened it, he told his friend Bundy that if it was not successful they could drink all the booze themselves. *Pete Esthus Collection. Courtesy of the Sarasota County History Center.*

nightclub in the old John Ringling Hotel. She died in 1968 in Venice and is buried in the Sandy Lane Pet Cemetery. Her grave marker reads, "Sleep well my darling companion. You will always be remembered."

CASH-STRAPPED COUNTY

In October 1940, the cash-strapped Sarasota County government found it necessary to borrow $25,000 at 6 percent interest to pay operating costs. The Palmer Bank loaned $15,000, and $5,000 was loaned by the Sarasota State Bank and Venice-Nokomis Bank. The county expected to be able to begin repayment when the December tax payments began arriving.

BOMBER CRASH

The Ninety-seventh Bomb Group of the Eighth Army Air Force, which trained in Sarasota in B-17s, participated in America's first air raids

When the Sarasota Army Air Base proved inadequate for the heavy bombers, training was switched to fighter planes. Here, Colonel James Ferguson, commanding officer of the Sarasota Army Air Base, flies his P-40. *Longboat Key Historical Society Collection. Courtesy of the Sarasota County History Center.*

over Europe. However, the runway for the heavy bombers proved to be inadequate, and there were many accidents. One such accident occurred on June 12, 1942, when a bomber crashed in Sarasota Bay, just south of Whitfield Estates, killing eight and injuring two.

The base was later converted to P-40 fighter training.

According to Bob Widner, 941 planes and 1,902 lives were lost in Florida through training-related accidents.

HONOR PARKWAY

In 1943, the Founders Circle of the Sarasota Garden Club appointed a committee to determine a suitable memorial to honor the men and women of Sarasota County who were overseas fighting in World War II.

Mrs. Edward W. Pinkham, who chaired the committee, came up with the idea of Honor Parkway, a living memorial of lovely *Cocos plumosas* trees on Bayfront Park, south of the Municipal Auditorium, to honor both those who would be lost in battle, as well as those who would be lucky enough to return home.

On a bright January day in 1947, the community came together, joined by the American Legion, the AMVETS color guard and the Sarasota High School marching band, to listen to speeches recalling the difficult war years, offer prayers and, most importantly, to thank and pay their respects to their hometown heroes. Each of the trees was decorated with a green-and-white wreath.

Master of Ceremonies Frank Evans, a local World War II naval officer, introduced the speakers. Founders Circle president Mrs. Walter G. Frauenheim told the audience that the parkway would be "a place of sanctity...in our busy little city" and that "the city and the public [would] assist in maintaining it as such." Civic leader Karl Bickel reminded onlookers, "We must as a community, never forget that a living memorial involves a keen and sensitive sense of community responsibility."

Mayor J. Douglas Arnest then came forward to accept the parkway for the city, and City Manager Ross Windom promised that the city would maintain the parkway and the trees.

Perhaps the most poignant part of the ceremony was when Sarasota High School principal Carl C. Strode presented a plaque with the names of graduated students who were killed during the war.

The 1940s

The ceremony ended with a twenty-one-gun salute followed by taps.

Sadly, the flush of patriotism and sentiment waned for Honor Parkway, just as it had for the Memorial Oaks on upper Main Street, which was uprooted in the mid-1950s.

The "community sense of responsibility" that Bickel had spoken of dissolved with time. He had warned, "We cannot enthusiastically accept this gift today and walk away and forget it tomorrow." But that seems to be precisely what happened.

Two of the trees and a plaque remain; you can see them at the headquarters of the Sarasota Garden Club. They serve as reminders for only a very few who recall that sentimental January day so many years ago.

REMEMBERING LONGBOAT KEY

One of Sarasota's most prominent architects, Edward J. "Tim" Seibert, reminisced about Longboat Key in an interview, "A Conversation with Tim Seibert," for *Clubhouse Magazine* in May 1980:

> *When I first knew Longboat, the middle of it was a bombing and strafing range for the Army Air Corps. They'd stop traffic out there to wait until the planes had done their thing.*
>
> *In the 1940s, when I'd sail out to Long Beach at the north end, it was like a great adventure. The water was cleaner, there were more fish, the clouds were beautiful—it was just a beautiful piece of nature then.*
>
> *It was also a much harder life. Air conditioning wasn't everywhere, and mosquitoes were. By the time you got to September, if you didn't have a skin disease, well I considered it highly unusual.*
>
> *My father built out there in 1949, and I always thought of it as a wild tropical island. Now I'm playing a considerable role in its development, and, yes, that gives me a lot to think about. I honestly don't know what I would do if I could turn back the hands of time on Longboat.*
>
> *But I can't. Where once it was an island of eagles and mangroves and trees, it will now be a manicured manmade place. Where once it was in the hands of nature, now it's in the hands of man, and we have to do the very best job we can of it.*
>
> *That's what everyone doesn't seem to understand. If nature is going to stay—on Longboat or anywhere else—it is only because man wants it to, in*

such things as bird sanctuaries and mangrove protection laws, for example.
But that grand wild place of nature that it once was…well it's gone, man,
gone forever. Everyone who lives on Longboat has helped displace it.

BREAKING THROUGH THE GLASS CEILING

The first Sarasota woman to break through the local political glass ceiling was Miss Charlie Hagerman, who won the election for tax collector in 1944. She bested five male candidates in the primary and went on to defeat Mrs. Mary Chapman in the general election. At $7,500 per year, it was one of the highest-paying political jobs in the county. "Miss Charlie," as she was affectionately known, was described as "blond and charming," a hard worker known for her "tact and business management."

When she died of a heart attack in 1975, she had been at the job for thirty years and was remembered by former mayor Jack Betz as "a lovely, gentle person who took her position very seriously." During her tenure, the county's tax roll jumped from $596,238 in 1945, when she took office, to $2.8 billion in 1975.

THE 1950s

It was a kind of innocent time. Sarasota was very unstructured, very casual, not trying to be something—it was something. The people were themselves and there weren't pretensions. Mrs. McLean [Evelyn Walsh McLean of Hope diamond and *Washington Post* fame] *played poker with the ice man; it was a very casual atmosphere.*

Society was just a lot more simple in those days and there was a lot of optimism and a lot of positive thinking. We had people from all walks of life, some very artistic people, really a very eclectic group. And the city itself was pristine. There were flowers everywhere.
—Robert Carr, *Sarasota attorney, describing Sarasota in the 1950s in an interview with Pat Buck,* Sarasota Style, *April 3, 1994*

BROTHER CAN YOU SPARE A SPACE?

Parking in downtown Sarasota had not always been a problem. Issues began when the automobile replaced the horse and mule as the favored means of transport.

In the old days, the long-ago days when folks came into town to load up their horse-drawn wagons or carts with supplies—feed, grain, lumber and maybe a jar of white lightning—they simply pulled to the front of Turner and Company on lower Main Street, loaded their goods and said giddyap. The problem wasn't where to tie up the buckboard, it was what the horses frequently left behind.

When Dr. C.B. Wilson sputtered into town in 1909 in his Reo roadster (twenty horsepower of pure locomotion), maybe to go to Badger's Drugs at Five Points for some medicines and pharmaceutical supplies, his only problem was to watch where he stepped. With all the horses about, one couldn't be too careful.

But in the early 1920s, Sarasota was "discovered" as a vacation destination, and Henry Ford's Model-Ts were being turned out in prodigious numbers for ever-decreasing prices—practically everyone owned one. Thereafter, parking and problem went hand in hand like scotch and soda. It has remained so to this day.

In 1926, a real estate man up from Miami to check out Sarasota's real estate market (imagine that) commented that he knew Sarasota was a thriving city because he had to circle Main Street four times to find an open parking space. Photographs of those freewheeling yesteryears invariably show that downtown, particularly during the winter season, was jammed with black cars lining both sides of the street, while others circled the business district searching for a place to pull in.

The "off-season" always offered some respite to the locals as Sarasota reverted to its sleepy-town pace and relaxed lifestyle. Businesses typically closed their doors by noon on Wednesdays. It was summertime, and if the living was easy so, too, was the parking.

With the post–World War II boom, it was obvious that the problem of where shoppers, theatre-goers, diners and elbow-benders could conveniently park needed to be addressed.

In the mid-1950s, the matter became quite contentious. When the city suggested that it would buy downtown property to transform into off-street parking, E.S. Brown, who operated his own parking lots, railed that "the action would be a definite step toward socialism." He called for merchants to join together "in a cooperative type parking operation." Brown owned eight lots and contended that it had been proven that private enterprise was in a better position to create parking than city government. He didn't feel that tax payers' dollars should foot the bill to benefit a few downtown merchants. Fortunately, it was not necessary to call out the National Guard to prevent this first step down the slippery slope toward socialism.

At the beginning of 1956, one popular store owner, S.C. "Bud" Montgomery, president of Montgomery-Roberts on Pineapple Avenue, offered one hour of free parking to customers who presented their stamped receipts to Mac, the parking lot attendant. Montgomery-Roberts shoppers were happy shoppers.

In January 1956, downtown merchants presented a petition to the city (city government *loves* petitions) requesting parking meters in front of their stores to hurry along those who pulled into a space at eight in the morning and didn't leave until a week and a half later. Approximately 110 new meters were purchased for Pineapple and Palm Avenues and the South Tamiami Trail, with 50 more meters slated for the area around Herald Square. Police officers driving Good Humor–white, three-wheeled Harley Davidson motorcycles handed out tickets to those who overstayed their nickel. (By contrast, in 1926, at the behest of the chamber of commerce, police officers were told to put "welcoming cards" on the windows of out-of-state visitors, telling them that they could park any place and for any length of time they wished until "they became acquainted with the various city ordinances.")

Some merchants feared that the meters would decrease their business and petitioned to have them removed. Other merchants, upset that some people were parking, willy-nilly, everywhere, requested No Parking signs, and the owner of a rooming house wanted the police to shoo cars away from the front of her establishment.

With the opening of Ringling Shopping Center in 1955 and Southgate Shopping Center in 1956, each with parking aplenty, coupled with the outward spread to the country, the downtown parking woes should have been diminished. They weren't—more and more people were moving here permanently.

Mr. Brown's protestations notwithstanding, the city continued to seek out space for the sleek, overly chromed chariots and station wagons of the day. In February, the city expressed interest in two downtown lots on First Street recommended by City Manager Ken Thompson. This added 275 more off-street spaces, but it wouldn't be enough.

In 1960, the notion of how cars should be parked was revisited—diagonal or parallel? In the 1950s, parallel parking had replaced the angle parking of the '20s, '30s and '40s. Since all else had failed, the city decided to reexamine the issue. R.W. Pavitt, the city planning director, thought it was a waste of time and money and said that the merchants would come to regret it. Angle parking, he said, caused accidents when drivers backed into moving traffic.

After a three-month trial period, which ended in January 1961 and proved Pavitt right, Mayor M.E. Marable announced after the unanimous vote, "And so dies angle parking."

Reports of its demise were premature—perhaps wishful thinking. As we know today, swerving away from cars backing out in front of us is part of the downtown experience; it takes a neck the length of a giraffe's to stretch far enough to see beyond myriad pickup trucks and SUVs as we inch blindly into oncoming traffic.

UNITED NATIONS FLAG

On July 24, 1950, the United Nations flag was raised over the city at the American Legion Memorial flagpole at Five Points. One thousand spectators showed up for the occasion, which "brought Sarasota the distinction of becoming the first city in the nation to signify its allegiance to the high aims of world peace and friendship symbolized by the United Nations."

But the flag incurred the wrath of the Disabled American Veterans Association, which reminded everyone that Russia, a UN member, was supplying arms to North Korea, a nation that we were fighting.

A GUILTY CONSCIENCE

In February 1950, county school superintendent Verman Kimbrough received a letter with a quarter in it and a request for forgiveness. It seems that in 1938, as a Fruitville Elementary School pupil, the letter writer had swiped a red pencil. The deed had been troubling her conscience ever since. She said, "I ask forgiveness for the sin I committed many years ago. Even though it may seem very small, a sin is a sin in God's sight and must be forgiven before we can have real peace."

Mr. Kimbrough responded, "Your action is so fine it will be publicized and may make some child think before he does something he might be sorry for later."

The quarter went into a fund to buy pencils for students.

THE SARASOTA QUEEN

In January 1951, a B-29 bomber, christened the *Sarasota Queen* (named to honor the hometown of copilot Jimmie J. Stewart's girlfriend, Orine Nelson

Yent, who later married him), dedicated a bombing mission over Korea to the folks of Sarasota. During a public relations tour, the crew was invited to Sarasota, where they were treated to a hero's welcome and put up at Florasota Gardens.

The *Sarasota Queen* dropped 1.6 million tons of bombs, the most bombs during the Korean War, and is now in the Air Force Museum in Akron, Ohio.

Major Stewart and his wife settled in Sarasota, where he became president of Florida Sun Realty. He died in 1998.

DEVELOPING BIRD KEY

Preceding Arvida's development of Bird Key, the Ringling interests planned a three-hundred-acre development using the surrounding submerged lands. John Ringling had acquired Bird Key in the 1920s, and his sister Ida Ringling lived in the Worcester Mansion until she died in December 1950.

The Ringlings' New York attorneys spelled out their plans, calling for a "high grade residential area," creating numerous inlets and basins to achieve the greatest number of waterfront lots.

But the plan was not well received, and at a particularly acrimonious meeting, wherein it was implied by the attorneys that a member of the city commission opposing the project had a feud with some of the Ringling family, Representative James Haley rose angrily to his feet and lambasted, "What do you mean coming here with this curbside gossip? You can't come down here and tell us how to run our affairs. Why don't you go back to New York and run your own business."

"Mr. Sarasota," A.B. Edwards added, "When you interfere with the channels, bars, currents and water ways you're liable to have trouble." He indicated that it would be easy to spoil the looks of the bay, considered, he said, "to be the most beautiful bay in America."

The development of Bird Key would have to wait for another time and another proposal.

MOBILE HOMES

The Fourth Annual Mobile-Home Exposition, held at the Municipal Auditorium, reportedly drew 150,000 people in three days.

Abe Namey, who singlehandedly developed the popular Southwinds Mobile Homes Park on the South Trail near Stickney Point Road in the early 1950s, relaxes against his Ford Ranchero. A former PT boat crewman during World War II, Namey also owned the Brooke to Bay Trailer Park in Englewood. He died on November 26, 2000. *Author's collection.*

The Miss Mobile Home Park Queen that year was slated to get a TV and modeling contract, plus a trip to Havana. The prizes were won by Jane Snyder, with Mrs. Peter Piper crowned the Most Glamorous Grandma. Both lived in the Gulfshore Trailer City on Longboat Key.

In explaining why trailer registrations jumped from 94 in 1947 to 3,283 in 1954, it was noted that the ten-dollars-a-year license tag was all the taxes that trailer owners paid.

THE UNIDENTIFIED DRIVING OBJECT

The mystery of the unidentified driving object was solved by the *News*, which explained that the odd-looking vehicle was a 1954 Mercedes Benz, an automobile purchased by William Selby through Cutler Motors. The diesel engine car got forty-seven miles per gallon. Selby explained that, speed-wise, it was "an old man's car."

COMFORTABLE CLIMATE

In the mid-1950s, when Sarasota was advertising itself as the Air-Conditioned City, locals were told that while New Yorkers were broiling in 100-degree August weather, it was a cool 87.5 here. Thinking of going to Washington, D.C.? Well, it was 98 degrees there.

SARASOTA CHARM

Writing for the *News* in May 1955, Professor Ellis Freeman, who had been vacationing in Sarasota since the 1930s and who built the Four Seasons Apartments on Ben Franklin Drive, wrote of the charm and atmosphere of the area:

> *The town had the tone and charm of a fishing village. No one was ever disturbed by the slightly ominous note of tax sales as they skipped merrily on at the courthouse. Artists and writers and professors like myself loved it for the complete absence of resort commercialism. It was what one hoped to find on Cape Cod and never did.*

He noted that in construction of the Four Seasons:

> *We probably alienated the entire local land-clearing and bulldozing industry, for we did not knock over a single tree either in erecting our buildings or cutting the road. Indeed no bulldozer showed its ugly face on the premises during all the building operations.*

OLD ENOUGH TO BOWL

In October 1955, the Sarasota City Commission allowed young people between ages fifteen and twenty-one to bowl in a commercial bowling alley. An ordinance passed in 1924, which forbade bowling by that age group, was overturned. However, the commission turned down a request by the owner of the Pastime Pool Room to allow those under eighteen to enter a pool hall.

MISCREANT YOUTH

While the city was voting about where local teens could and could not hang out, the Siesta Drive-In was screening *High School Sin*, "The Naked Truth About the Dangerous Generation." On the same bill was a "Sensational Exposé of the Dope Racket," *The Marihuana Story* about "Girl Gangs Hopped Up."

Throughout the 1950s, juvenile delinquency was big news as young people turned to godless rock and roll, the scourge of the American way, much as jazz and syncopated rhythms were considered the downfall of the sheiks and flappers of the Roaring Twenties.

Mainstream Hollywood put out a number of such worrisome flicks as *Rebel Without a Cause*, with James Dean and Sal Mineo, and *The Wild One*, with Marlon Brando, underscoring America's concern for miscreant youth.

HOUSING DEVELOPMENTS

The mid-1950s was a time of notable growth in housing developments. Greenbriar Estates, off of Tuttle Avenue, offered the first "moderately" priced split-level homes for $13,750 and, in November 1955, sold twenty-three of them the first week.

Sarasota Springs offered homes for $6,995 and lots for $895, advertising "Nature Was Smiling When She Made Sarasota Springs."

Lake Sarasota had lots from $595.

South Gate, "Where You Live Among the Orange Blossoms," offered homes for $15,000.

DeSoto Lakes offered its "Designed For You" homes for $6,995 and $7,995 and homesites, "plenty of them," for $695, with 25 percent down and three years to pay.

The developer of Bay Shore listed six essentials for a successful Florida housing development:

1. A screened area
2. Sliding glass doors
3. A built-in range and oven
4. A blend of architecture
5. Adequate maintenance of the development
6. Inclusion of a recreation center

Interestingly, an air conditioner was not listed. Bay Shore's White Orchid model—two bedrooms, one bath *and* a swimming pool—was offered at $13,990.

Those inclined to trailer life had many choices available. By the mid-1950s, it was estimated that there were thirty trailer parks in the county. Trailer Estates offered a forty- by sixty-foot lot for fifteen dollars per month, which would be paid off "in about four years." One of the fringe benefits was the community TV antenna.

The manager of the City Mobile Park, Martin O'Neill, offered the following to explain the popularity of trailer life: "I think it's because of the greater fellowship that's possible in a trailer camp. We've got more retired people here and fewer young people."

BUNDY AND EVANS RETIRE

Two announcements, printed within a day of each other, signaled the retirement of two local celebrities who enjoyed international renown. On December 11, 1955, Rudy Bundy, a thirty-year bandsman who had come to Sarasota to open the storied Lido Casino, announced that he was quitting music to take the position of sales and marketing manager for Ringling Bros. and Barnum & Bailey Circus. Bundy, who was a good friend of John Ringling North, had played throughout the country during the Big Band era and in Sarasota at the Casa Madrid, Manhattan and Tropical Lounges, as well as at the M'ToTo Room, where he entertained for seven years. (As Bundy told the story of the popular M'ToTo Room, one night he and North went to John Ringling's old real estate office on St. Armands Circle, broke into the musty place for a look-see and determined that it wasn't large enough for their purposes. The next stop for the duo was the John Ringling Hotel, which North would imbue with the trappings of the circus. It was here where he decided to open the M'ToTo Room lounge, telling Bundy that if it didn't work out they could drink all the booze themselves. But the M'ToTo Room quickly became a hit, for many years the focal point of Sarasota's nightlife, with Bundy playing his "sizzling clarinet," occasionally accompanied by North.)

Bundy later served the circus as vice-president and treasurer and was on the board of directors until he retired in 1970. He died on August 1, 2000, at age ninety-three.

On December 12, 1955, Merle Evans retired from his job as leader of the Ringling Circus Band after thirty-seven years with the Greatest Show on Earth. He had joined in 1919 and played twenty-two thousand performances without missing a show.

His retirement was not long lasting, however, and he soon returned to the big top. In 1966, Sarasota put on a two-day Merle Evans Days, replete with a circus parade and local dignitaries, to honor the great showman and musician who at that time had forty-six years with the circus. He ultimately retired in 1969, still not missing a show or even being late for one. It was estimated that he played before 165 million people, more than any other person in history.

Merle, who lived to be ninety-five, died on December 31, 1987.

THE CIRCUS HALL OF FAME

Sarasota's relationship to the circus was underscored when the Circus Hall of Fame opened on January 8, 1955. The building and grounds showcased a vast collection of circus memorabilia and offered live circus acts. It was billed as a Shrine to Stars. Its centerpiece was the ten-ton Two Hemispheres Band Wagon, built in 1896 for Phineas T. Barnum. It was said to have been found abandoned at the Iowa State Fairgrounds, where Colonel B.J. Palmer restored it and gave it to the Hall of Fame.

AIR CONDITIONING

It was prophesized in the *News* that 1955 would be a big year for air conditioning in Sarasota. The afternoon paper noted that two factors would contribute to the upturn in home air: 1) housewives were becoming used to shopping in air-conditioned stores and would not long tolerate coming home to swelter; and 2) the "bread winners" (their husbands), who worked in air-conditioned offices, would want the same comfort in their homes.

The 1950s

Plans for the Downtown Bay Front

At the beginning of 1956, a preliminary plan was put forth to the city commission by the planning board for the development of the downtown bay front at Gulf Stream Avenue. The sketch of the proposal was done by well-known architect William Zimmerman and called for skyscraper apartments to line the bay front and for Gulf Stream Avenue to be turned into "a promenade with shops running from the intersection of the North Trail south to Strawberry Avenue." It also offered a man-made island jutting into the bay and room for a modern marina, saltwater pool, water ski theatre, shops and a park.

Performance at the Florida Theatre

On February 21, 1956, Justin Tubb, the Louvin Brothers, Mother Maybelle and the Carter Sisters came to Sarasota for a live performance at the Florida Theatre. The matinée cost seventy-six cents for adults and fifty cents for children. Also present was a hip-gyrating fellow named Elvis Presley with the Blue Moon Boys.

Sarasota Writers, an Incomplete Account

In 1956, local author MacKinlay Kantor won the Pulitzer Prize for his Civil War epic, *Andersonville*. Kantor was one of many writers who found inspiration in Sarasota, still a slow-paced, tropical paradise with miles of unspoiled beaches, a relaxed lifestyle, a temperate climate and unassuming locals.

Renowned artists, sculptors, cartoonists and illustrators were drawn to this inviting Gulf Coast paradise in droves, and a group of local architects, known collectively as members of the Sarasota School of Architecture, derived international acclaim for their stunning, modernistic designs.

The Ringling Bros. and Barnum & Bailey Circus laid the foundation for much of the local color, with the trappings of the Greatest Show on Earth sprinkled throughout the community, and the never-ending parade of head-turning visitors has included royalty, sports figures, movie and television stars and well-known politicians, all adding to Sarasota's allure as a unique, go-to cultural haven.

Less visible was the colony of local writers. The group included some of the finest novelists, screenwriters, short-story writers, essayists and poets of their era.

For over thirty years, beginning in 1952, the august group of local literary types left their respective typewriters long enough to saunter downtown each Friday for lunch, mostly at the Plaza Restaurant, where they ate, drank, swapped stories, told ribald jokes and played liar's poker. It was a loosely federated gathering. As member Richard Glendinning noted in his account of the assemblage, concerning notification of attendance, "There are no officers and no one to notify. Attendance would indicate that you are probably there. Absence tends to suggest the opposite. In any case, no one will be altogether sure."

At one of their afternoon soirées, it was figured that between them they had published over three hundred books plus myriad short stories, magazine articles and screen plays. A shortlist of the Sarasota colony follows.

The above-mentioned MacKinlay Kantor moved here in 1936, already an established author. His first successful book, *Diversey*, was published in 1928, ending his "starving writer" status. Kantor, his wife Irene and their two children lived for many years on Siesta Key, where he worked in a study adorned with photographs attesting to his combat experiences as a decorated correspondent during World War II and Korea. Other photos show him with Hollywood luminaries (his book *The Best Years of Our Lives* was turned into a motion picture that won multiple Academy Awards), and there are numerous covers from the magazines in which his work appeared: the *Saturday Evening Post, Look, Collier's, True* and *Esquire*, to name a few. He once lived the life of a New York City patrolman to research the book *Signal 32*. *Andersonville* was a book he "dreamed about writing" for twenty-five years. It was hugely successful. A prolific writer, Kantor's other books include *I Love You, Irene, Spirit Lake, Valedictory, Gentle Annie* and numerous others.

Another Siesta Key resident, John D. MacDonald, moved to what was then still an unblemished tropical out-island in 1951. MacDonald wrote the masterful Travis McGee mystery series, which critics said proved "that popular fiction could be composed with intelligence and style." Among his seventy-five novels, *Condominium*, published in 1977, was a bestseller, awakening readers to the devastating effects of a huge hurricane hitting an over-developed, poorly constructed coastal community (some local readers thought his fictitious Fiddler Key was actually Siesta Key), taking on developers and dishonest politicians. The clash between preservationists and developers was the basis of *A Flash of Green*, and he put televangelists under the hot lamp with *One More Sunday*. His novel *The Executioner* became the popular 1962 film *Cape Fear*, starring Gregory Peck and Robert Mitchum. (It was remade in 1991.) MacDonald once said that he wrote primarily to entertain and quoted Sam Goldwyn's witticism, "If you want to send a message, call Western Union."

Venice resident Walter Farley came to the area in 1946 and authored a series of twenty-one Black Stallion books. A lifelong horse lover, his first book was started while he was still in high school and was published in 1941. After he returned from World War II, the first sequel, *The Black Stallion Returns*, was published. The adventure stories of Alec Ramsey and the fantastic stallion captivated young people around the world and sold millions of copies in over twenty countries. *The Black Stallion* was made into a movie, directed by Francis Ford Coppola, and garnered two Academy Award nominations. A *New Yorker* magazine writer said that it might have been the greatest children's movie ever made. Farley died in 1989 of a heart attack, but his books still remain popular.

Another regular at the Friday luncheons was novelist, playwright, producer, director and screenwriter Joseph Hayes, who began wintering in Sarasota with his family on Lido Shores in the mid-1950s. The winner of two Tony Awards and the Edgar Allan Poe Award from the Mystery Writers of America, Hayes's 1955 *Desperate Hours* was a novel, Broadway production starring Paul Newman and Karl Malden and film-noir classic motion picture with Humphrey Bogart and Fredric March. Other movies from Hayes include *The Young Doctors* and productions for Disney films and television shows. In 1975, Hayes directed one of his plays, *Impolite Comedy*, at the Golden Apple Dinner Theatre.

Besides being one of the best-known artists and illustrators of his day, Ben Stahl, another Siesta Key resident, was also an author. His novel *Blackbeard's Ghost* was made into a Disney movie starring Peter Ustinov in 1968. The book was billed as a "hilarious rib rattling ghost story." He also wrote *Secret of Red Skull*. Longtime Sarasota residents may remember Stahl's Museum of the Cross, which opened with great fanfare in 1966, where he displayed his fifteen mural-sized paintings of the Way of the Cross. The museum was robbed of the paintings, valued at over $1 million in 1969. They have never been recovered. Stahl, who moved to Siesta Key in 1953, died in 1987.

Sarasota Herald-Tribune journalist Charlie Huisking noted that Borden Deal wrote novels about the New South "with poignancy and passion." His

Dunbar's Cove, translated into twenty languages, told the story of the creation of the Tennessee Valley Authority and its sweeping effects on the rural population. It was filmed as *Wild River*, starring Montgomery Clift and Lee Remick. Deal, who moved to Sarasota in 1964, also wrote *Bluegrass*, which was turned into a two-part miniseries on CBS; *The Tobacco Men*, based on the life of J.B. Hughes, who started the American Tobacco Company; and *A Long Way to Go*, an adventure story about three stranded children who must use their own devices to get home. Deal's wife, Babs, was also a novelist and short story writer. Deal was only sixty-two when he died of a heart attack in 1985.

Prolific playwright Irving Vendig and his wife, Phyllis, came to Sarasota in 1938. Both were script writers, he being a pioneer in television soap operas, creating the daytime soap *The Edge of Night*, which ran for almost thirty years. He wrote over two thousand scripts for the Perry Mason radio show and the pilot for the TV version of show and created the "Judy and Dick" radio series, which aired for twenty-five years. He also wrote many scripts for *Search for Tomorrow*. Vendig did most of his writing in Sarasota and commuted to Chicago, New York and Burbank to work on the programs. He said of his writing, "It's practically an eight-day-a-week job. You couldn't stand the pressures if you didn't enjoy the work." Vendig died in 1995 at age ninety-two.

Most of yesteryear's famous Sarasota authors have moved on or passed on. The storied Plaza Restaurant on First Street, which hosted them for so many years, closed its doors a long time ago. And while Sarasota still has a cadre of fine writers—Stephen King, Bob Plunkett and Stuart Kaminsky come immediately to mind—the city with the inspirational blend of beauty and tranquility that drew so many of them belongs to a bygone era.

PARTY LINES

At the end of 1956, the Peninsula Telephone Company switched to a new numbering system and offered four exchanges: RIngling (naturally) for the main city area; ELgin for the north side; FUlton for St. Armands, Lido and Longboat; and EXport for Sarasota Beach. At the time, the number of phones had risen to 17,530, up from 3,149 in 1940, 4,475 in 1945 and 9,162 in 1950.

The company also offered tips to being a courteous party line neighbor:

1. Hang up the receiver carefully after each call.
2. Use the line "sharingly" allowing five minutes between each call.

3. Give up the line immediately in an emergency.
4. Keep all calls reasonably brief.

The reward for such stellar phone behavior? "Better party line service for yourself and everyone."

South Gate Shopping Center

When South Gate Shopping Center was officially opened on January 15, 1957, the ribbon-cutting ceremony included Mayor A. Ray Howard, who lauded it as "another manifestation of the growth which is well known as a distinguishing characteristic of Sarasota."

Reportedly costing $1.5 million, the nineteen-store shopping center was described as "a glittering emporium of merchandising."

According to the *Sarasota Herald-Tribune*, "Beautiful girls in shorts passed through the jam packed stores pressing samples, free gifts and all sorts of coupons into the hands of the eager shoppers."

Prizes for the excited crowd included a sixteen-foot boat with a thirty-five-horsepower Evinrude motor, a $1,500 Hotpoint kitchen, twenty portable televisions and thirty transistor radios.

Polio Vaccine

One of the great fears faced by Sarasota parents and parents around the world was that their child might be stricken by polio, a disease whose origins no one seemed to know, nor whom it would strike next.

Children were particularly vulnerable. And the thought that one's child might be relegated to an iron lung to help him breathe or have his legs bound in braces so that he could walk was indeed anxiety provoking. (The iron lung was a large metal cylinder often likened to a coffin. It worked like a bellows, extending a push-pull motion on the chest to help the patient breath. Although confinement in an iron lung was dreaded, it did save lives.)

Ironically, it would be determined that it was improved sanitary conditions that prevented children from being exposed to small amounts of the virus, which previously had made them resistant to the disease.

The first major outbreak of polio in the United States was in 1894, but it was not until 1908 that the polio virus was first identified. The polio virus inflamed nerves in the brain and spinal cord, causing paralysis of the muscles in the chest, legs or arms. Severe cases needed the iron lung to help them breath.

The most famous person to be stricken was Franklin D. Roosevelt, who contracted the disease in 1921. When Roosevelt died in April 1945, he was honored by having his image placed on the dime. It was the National Foundation for Infantile Paralysis that used the March of Dimes campaign to raise funds to combat the disease.

The epidemic grew worse each year. In 1933, five thousand new cases were reported. By 1952, that number had grown to fifty-nine thousand.

Relief finally came in 1955 with the introduction of the vaccine developed by Jonas Salk. He was hailed as a miracle worker and refused to patent his vaccine, as he did not want to profit from his discovery.

Whereas the Salk vaccine was administered through an injection, usually in the upper arm, Dr. Albert Sabin developed a vaccine that could be taken orally. The advantage of the Sabine vaccine over the Salk is that it provides lifelong immunity, without the need of booster shots.

The local papers carried human interest stories of children getting their first inoculations, which began on April 20, 1955, much to the relief of parents. A typical picture with caption showed a smiling youngster standing next to his mother and looking up at the doctor: "MAMA EXPLAINS—Jimmy Fulton listens attentively as his mother, Mrs. W.E. Fulton, explains why he will be given a shot of the Salk polio vaccine and that it won't hurt a bit." Right.

MIDGET CITY, FLORIDA

You can almost hear the kids in the backseat of the family station wagon, "Daddy, are we there yet? Hmmm? Are we? Are we?"

It is the mid-1950s, the long-ago days before the Oompa-Loompas of Willy Wonka's chocolate factory but after the Munchkins of *The Wizard of Oz*, and "there" was to have been Midget City, Florida, a unique tourist attraction off U.S. 41, three miles south of the Sarasota city limits. The kids could probably hear members of the Lullaby League singing, "We wish to welcome you to Munchkinland."

At least that was the dream of Mrs. Neal Chapline Swalm, a local writer and promoter whose whimsical vision of Midget City was grand, in a suitably small-scale sort of way.

By the 1950s, various tourist attractions had spread throughout Sarasota County: Horn's Cars of Yesterday, the Ringling Art Museum and Cà d'Zan, the Glass Blowers, Texas Jim Mitchell's Animal Farm and the largest and most popular in all of Florida, the winter headquarters of the Ringling Bros. and Barnum & Bailey Circus. These would soon be joined in the late 1950s and early 1960s by the Circus Hall of Fame, Sunshine Springs and Gardens and Florida Land.

Mrs. Swalm, who had twenty-five years of publicity and promotion work to her credit, came up with the idea while interviewing "Midget Impresario" Nate Eagle for a book she was writing about his life's work of managing little people in such places as the Midget Village at the California Pacific International Exposition in San Diego in 1935 and "midget cities" in other fairs and expositions, as well as in Hollywood.

In the 1930s and 1940s, Eagle managed a troupe of over one hundred little people, including Dottie Williams, "Hollywood's Brightest Little Star," who was also known as "the Miniature Rita Hayworth"; Dot Wenzel, the "Tiniest Singing & Dancing Personality"; Trinidad Rodriguez, "the Smallest Woman in the World"; and numerous others.

Small-scale "towns" and other venues showcasing little people were nothing new and were very popular. General Tom Thumb (Sherwood Edward Stanton) toured in Europe with legendary showman P.T. Barnum, and his marriage to the diminutive Lavinia Warren was front-page news in 1863. Hollywood made a go of the public's fascination with people of small stature with the 1938 western *The Terror of Tiny Town*, and of course one of the most popular segments of *The Wizard of Oz* included the colorfully costumed Munchkins. *Three Wise Fools*, produced in 1946, included some of the Eagle troupe as leprechauns.

Sarasota was still the Circus City in those days and would have been a natural for Midget City. Members of the Doll family, who toured with Ringling Bros., were well known in the area, and it was generally, but incorrectly, believed that they lived in a doll-sized house that John Ringling built for them. Circus clown dwarfs had lived and worked in Sarasota since the late 1920s.

Mrs. Swalm noted that her vision of a Midget City would be unique—a type of Munchkinland. The only thing remotely close to it at the time

The Doll family. Left to right: Grace, Daisy, Tiny and Harry. Their reaction to the proposed Midget City is not known. *Pete Esthus Collection. Courtesy of the Sarasota County History Center.*

was a minor-league touring midget city that traveled from town to town in Europe.

Midget City, Florida, was to be incorporated and have all the amenities one would expect to find in any other township. The forty-acre tract of land on which it would be built would have

> *streets, sidewalks, street lighting, sewers, motels, a hotel, restaurant, church, theatre, golf course, swimming pool, shops, homes, restaurant, grocery store, barber shop, parking area, and miniature farm (with miniature animals), producing miniature vegetables and fruits.*

Of course, Midget City was to be inhabited totally by little people, who would run their own fire department and police department and elect their own mayor. Their chamber of commerce, too, would be composed of little people.

Although at the time Eagle did not have the vast number of little people under his supervision as he did in his heyday, Swalm proposed that an invitation be sent out to all the little people of the world "who were of sound mind and body" offering them an opportunity to spend their winters in Midget City or retire there, rent-free. They would be paid from proceeds of the holding corporation or by establishing their own concessions. No doubt, the Lollypop Guild would have done quite well.

For those who would be drawn to visit the attraction, Swalm suggested that a motel that could accommodate "normal-sized" people be built on the property.

The whole shebang would be supervised by Eagle. Swalm noted Eagle's bona fides for such an operation:

> [He] *has successfully operated enterprises such as this on a smaller scale, consisting as much as a quarter of a million dollars to construct, at fairs such as the Chicago World's Fair. Each of these like attractions were amortized in less than one year and showed a substantial profit.*

At the Midget Farm at the California Exposition, in which little people lived and worked for two years growing miniature fruit and vegetables, Eagle had procured miniature animals from all over the world.

Swalm bragged that of the four hundred known little people in the United States, "Mr. Eagle has worked with over 50% of them, knows them well, and is considered by them to be their champion in whom they have implicit trust." She insisted that he would have no trouble employing as many little people as it would take to run Midget City on a year-round basis.

The prospectus indicated that the entire project could be brought in for $290,000, including the cost of the forty acres of land pegged at "$44,000; city layout, $54,000; municipal buildings, $50,000; landscaping and architect's fee $22,000." The balance included these operating costs:

> *Midget salaries of $52,000 for forty midgets @ $100 per week for 13 weeks; two secretaries (presumably of normal height) $6,000; director Eagle's salary of $10,000; and other miscellaneous expenses, including Swalm's salary of $5,000.*

Income was projected to return 33.33 percent after amortization from such sources as a miniature art store, camera shop, fruit stand, Western Union, grocery store, barbershop, cocktail lounge, restaurant, shoe shop, dress shop, gasoline station, et cetera, depending only on one's imagination. Income would also be derived from miniature baskets of miniature fruits and vegetables; a sightseeing bus fare of ten cents a person; and a corporate-owned theatre to present a fifteen-minute "midget variety show" every hour for an adult admission of twenty-five cents and ten cents for children, who would also pay to ride a "midget train" and visit an amusement park with a "midget merry-go-round" and "midget Ferris wheel."

But that was only the beginning. She claimed that TV revenue would bolster the bottom line, plus the sale of children's garments could be astronomical. As Swalm put it, "It is a known fact that all little girls from about two to ten years love to 'play lady,' to dress up in their mother's clothes." Swalm and Eagle envisioned duplicating the clothes worn by the little people, which "could conceivably run into millions of dollars if promoted properly." She noted that Shirley Temple dresses had made a fortune.

The proposed location for Midget City was important. Situated on South U.S. 41, it would be directly on the path of those heading to and from Miami. The attraction would be marked by a huge arch noting No Admission and Free Parking.

Inasmuch as the winter headquarters, which was out of the way and difficult to find, had 200,000 paid admissions in 1954, Swalm asked, "How many more would enter Midget City when it stares them in the face?" In her view, at least, a lot more.

It is lost to history why the plan never materialized, but the next time you drive south of Bee Ridge Road, look over to the west. Among the myriad car lots and restaurants, there could be a place called Midget City filled with little people, and you could say to your children, "Well, kids here we are."

SHERIFF ROSS BOYER

In 1954, Sheriff Ross E. Boyer employed a staff of thirteen: five full-time deputies, two night officers, two Sunday officers, two school officers and two women working in the office. With this, he kept the peace over an area that covered 586 square miles and had a population of forty-two thousand.

Boyer, who had been with the Florida Highway Patrol, was elected to office as a Democrat four times beginning in 1952 on the campaign slogan "No friends to reward, no enemies to punish."

August 24, 1972, was proclaimed Sheriff Ross Boyer Day to honor the man who had "respected law and maintained order here for 20 years." He had to retire that year because of health reasons.

Rerouting U.S. 41

As the rerouting of U.S. 41 through beautiful Luke Wood Park and along the downtown bay front was nearing completion, the American Institute of Architects, some four hundred strong, was having its regional convention in Sarasota.

The meetings were covered in the *Sarasota Herald-Tribune* by Lawrence Dame, who reported that the group was bitterly unhappy with the result.

Paul Rudolph, stellar member of the Sarasota School of Architecture and chairman of the Department of Architecture at Yale, "decried the constantly progressing project for separating the center of the city from its greatest asset—the water." He felt that it was a desecration of natural resources.

More outspoken was Douglass Haskell, editor of the influential Architectural Forum. He remarked, "It's murder...I shout outrage...It's a filthy, dirty crime. It's unforgivable and idiotic, cutting off the community from where five years ago people could go to the pier and enjoy fishing and the bay."

Citizens who had opposed the project were criticized for not coming forward and making their feelings known to those responsible.

The old Ringling Bridge had seen better days by the time its replacement was completed in 1958. *Courtesy of the Sarasota County History Center.*

THE FALL OF THE OAKS

In what became a mid-1950s battle between oak trees and progress, with many longtime residents lining up squarely on the side of keeping the oaks, MacKinlay Kantor, Sarasota's Pulitzer Prize–winning author (*Andersonville*) wrote the following bit of sarcasm for the *Sarasota Herald* on January 23, 1955:

> *To The Editor,* Sarasota Herald-Tribune.
>
> *I am horrified at the attitude of the local garden clubs in opposing the destruction of the memorial oaks on Main Street. These misguided people cannot possibly understand the term progress. They refuse to recognize that Sarasota and Sarasota County are no longer a way of life; on the contrary they now constitute the most bustling lets-get-down-to-brass-tacks-put-your-shoulder-to-the-wheel commercial development in Florida. No longer do we wish to attract people from the North to move down here because they appreciate semi-rustic peace and wish to retain it unaltered. The plan, as I see it demonstrated, is to lure as many people as possible from Ohio and Michigan (preferably pensioners: the solid, substantial but far-seeing type) so they can move down here and expunge worthless oak trees and slay worthless mangroves in order to make room for more people from Ohio and Indiana to move down here in order to rip out unsightly Spanish moss in order to make room for more people from Indiana and Wisconsin to come down here and bulldoze ugly sea-grapes in order to make room for more people from Wisconsin and Michigan to hasten down and fill in disagreeable salt-water bays in order to make room for more people from Ohio to come here and— Excuse me. My traditional patience is exhausted at the stupidity of garden clubbers who wish to keep a few ridiculous trees on Main Street merely because they were planted as a memorial to some forgotten kids who died in a forgotten war. Why can't these people be Boosters for PROGRESS?*
>
> *MACKINLAY KANTOR, Siesta Key*

Sadly, over the protestations of many, including a group that was formed to save them (called Friends of Friendly Oaks), the oaks went down, one by one, all 181 of them; one planted for each Sarasota serviceman who heeded the call to fight in World War I. In so doing, the city broke the promise made by Woman's Club president Mrs. Frederick H. Guenther that they would provide "an avenue of living trees, whose beauty and grateful shade would delight and bless generations long after you had passed on."

Dean of Sarasota's colony of writers, Pulitzer Prize–winning author MacKinlay Kantor. A recreation of his office can be seen at the Sarasota County History Center. *Courtesy of the Sarasota County History Center.*

A LACK OF FISH

J.C. Tucker, who for over twenty-six years was the bridge tender for the Ringling Bridge, the area's busiest, complained about the lack of fish. "Why, in the old days it was nothing to catch 100 to 125 fish in a day," he lamented in 1956.

BE PREPARED!

In the 1950s, when the Civil Defense was suggesting atomic blast drills and folks were building bomb shelters in their backyards to stave off the effects of radiation in case of an attack, the *Bradenton Herald* announced that preparations were being made. The story ran on October 15, 1957, under the headline "If H-Bomb Wipes out Bradenton, Oneco Will Become County Seat." The plan, adopted at the Manatee County Commission meeting, proposed that if Bradenton was decimated, the school at Oneco would become home of county government. If that, too, were wiped out in a blast, Myakka was offered as an alternate site.

THE SOX AND SARASOTA

At the end of the 1958 spring training season, community leaders, major league ballplayers and six hundred baseball fans gathered for a celebration at the National Guard Armory. It was the silver anniversary of the relationship between Sarasota and the Boston Red Sox.

A broadly smiling Joe Cronin, the team general manager and former field general, accepted from Wayne Hibbs, of the chamber of commerce, a gift of twenty-five golf balls, while a beaming Mrs. Cronin was photographed holding a bouquet of flowers. A cake large enough for the occasion, with twenty-five candles for Cronin to blow out, was brought forward as the guests applauded. Even the usually reticent Ted Williams was on hand for the gala event to show a short film of him battling a 1,235-pound marlin.

When it was time for his speech, Cronin promised the gleeful assembly that the Sox would come back to Sarasota: "We have had 25 years of happy association with the people of Sarasota and have no intention of moving our training base to Arizona, California or anywhere else." Cronin

A young Ted Williams atop one of Texas Jim Mitchell's alligators. The "Splendid Stick" was a Sarasota favorite when the Boston Red Sox trained here until 1958. *Pete Esthus Collection. Courtesy of the Sarasota County History Center.*

then read a telegram from owner Tom Yawkey pledging to remain for the foreseeable future.

From the Great Depression into Sarasota's 1950s building resurgence, the Sox was *our* team. More than a few players made Sarasota their home, and the team's arrival each March for spring training was a major event. Indeed, the Sox had become an integral part of the fabric of Sarasota's recreational life, just as the circus, the Sara de Sota pageant, the Jungle Gardens and any number of other popular local attractions.

Unfortunately, the "foreseeable future" extended only until that June. The Sox threw the community a fast ball, high and inside, and it hit us right on the noggin. The *Sarasota Journal* compared the announcement to being bombed—a surprise attack; the Sox were walking in favor of Scottsdale, Arizona:

> *Chief bombardier locally was the Bosox' number one laughing boy and traveling secretary, genial Tom Dowd. But Dowd was all business yesterday as he scored a direct hit at City Manager Ken Thompson...Hit by the first pieces of shrapnel was Mayor Frank Hoestring* [and the city commissioners].

Community reaction was summed up by Dave Boylston, owner of Badger's Drugs: "I think it was a pretty raw deal to let us go ahead with this bond issue to get $100,000 to fix up Payne Park and on the spur of the moment to pull that kind of trick."

Since 1924, except for a few years during the beginning of the Depression and during World War II, when rail travel prohibited baseball travel below the Mason-Dixon line, Sarasota had a major league team, and the hunt for a replacement became a top priority.

Ken Thompson, along with chamber of commerce sports committee chairman Willie Robarts and chamber of commerce manager Tod Swalm, flew to the all-star game in Baltimore to pitch Sarasota to "one of the Big Sixteen."

The next day, Thompson reported that while no teams were available for spring training in 1959, the Brooklyn Dodgers had agreed to play some games in Sarasota. As the *Sarasota Journal* put it, "The Los Angeles Dodgers, those wonderful 'Bums' that formerly shot pool in Brooklyn will play at least nine games at Sarasota's Payne Park this coming spring." It was a stop-gap measure, but in 1960 Bill Veeck, the "Barnum of Baseball," would bring the "GoGo" Chicago White Sox, and again there was joy in Sarasotaville.

I.Z. MANN

I.Z. Mann's name should be as synonymous with contemporary Sarasota as Mira Mar Hotel builder Andrew McAnsh was to the 1920s. Coming up from Miami in 1959, Mann helped jump-start the condominium craze and is credited with building Sarasota's first major condominiums. One realtor recalled that Mann had to spell condominium phonetically on his for-sale signs so people here would know how to pronounce the word. Longtime real estate man and civic leader Parker Banzhaf was quoted as saying, "He had quite an impact on the community. He was a pioneer of condominium construction." He coined the word "condo-maximum," and his projects in Sarasota beginning in the 1960s were a harbinger of today's dramatic influx of downtown condominiums, which fueled our last frenetic real estate boom.

ALWAYS OPEN

When the new police station opened on Ringling Boulevard at the end of 1959, Chief Scott threw away the keys to the building, noting that it would always be open.

BIRD KEY LOTS

It was reported in the *News* on October 16, 1959, that the first person to buy a lot on Bird Key was Mrs. Marie G. Eppenberger, a real estate agent for St. Armands Real Estate. She waited all night at the Arvida office door from 10:00 p.m. to 8:00 a.m. A woman walking her dog passed by and asked Eppenberger what she was doing. When told about the Bird Key lots, the woman told Eppenberger to buy one for her, too.

Several hundred agents had attended the Arvida presentation at the Municipal Auditorium the afternoon before as four wheelbarrows, with a total of $500,000, were wheeled onstage to show the amount of commissions that would be available to brokers selling property on Bird Key.

The development was also plugged by TV personality Dave Garroway on his *Today* show.

SELECTED BIBLIOGRAPHY

Browning, Alex. "Memoirs," March 21, 1932. On file at the Sarasota County History Center.

Burns, Owen, and John Ringling. Telegrams. Provided to the author by Lillian Burns.

Curtis, Fannie Crocker. Interview by former Sarasota County historian Dottie Davis. On file at the Sarasota County History Center.

Edwards, A.B. Interview by former Sarasota County historian Dottie Davis, July 23, 1958. On file at the Sarasota County History Center.

Esthus, George I. "Pete." *A History of Agriculture of Sarasota County, Florida.* Sarasota County Agriculture Fair Association and the Sarasota County Historical Commission, 2003.

Gillespie, Blanche McDaniel. Interview with her nephew, Charles V. Swain Jr., 1955. Paper on file at the Sarasota County History Center.

Grismer, Karl H. *The Story of Sarasota.* M.E. Russell, 1946.

Haardt, Georges-Marie. "Through the Deserts and Jungles of Africa by Motor." *National Geographic* (June 1926).

Lawrie, Nellie. "The Scotch Colony Comes to Sarasota." Recollections on file at the Sarasota County History Center.

Marth, Del. *Yesterday's Sarasota.* Miami: E.A. Seemann Publishing, Inc., 1973.

McElroy, Annie M. *But Your World and My World: The Struggle For Survival, A Partial History of Blacks in Sarasota County, 1884–1986.* N.p.: Black South Press, 1986.

McKennon, Joe. *Rape of an Estate.* Self-published, 1986.

[The] *News*

North, Henry Ringling, and Alden Hatch. *The Circus Kings: Our Ringling Family Story.* Garden City, NY: Doubleday & Company, 1960.

Peeples, Vernon E. "The Sarasota Democratic Vigilantes." Paper on file at Sarasota County History Center.

Plowden, Gene. *Those Amazing Ringlings and their Circus.* New York: Bonanza Books, 1967.

Sarasota Herald-Tribune

Sarasota Magazine

Sarasota Origins. Historical Society of Sarasota County, Summer 1988.

Sarasota Times

Spears, Susan Roberts. *Assorted Tales and Other Lies.* N.p., 1993.

Weeks, David C. *Ringling: The Florida Years, 1911–1936.* Gainesville: University Press of Florida, 1993.

Whitaker, A.K. *One Man's Family (in Seven Parts).* Self-published. On file at the Sarasota County History Center.

ABOUT THE AUTHOR

Jeff LaHurd is the history specialist for Sarasota County. He and his wife, Jennifer, have four children and two grandchildren. Jeff grew up in Sarasota, attended school at St. Martha's and Cardinal Mooney and graduated from Sarasota High. He has a BA in history and an MA in rehabilitation counseling from the University of South Florida. He has written for *Sarasota Magazine*, *SRQ*, *Sarasota Downtown and Beyond*, the *Sarasota Herald-Tribune* and the *Sarasota Observer*. His video, *Sarasota: Landmarks of the Past*, was shown on the History Channel and won an award from the Florida Trust for Historic Preservation for outstanding contribution to preservation in the field of communication.

Other books by Jeff LaHurd:

Gulf Coast Chronicle: Remembering Sarasota's Past
Lido Casino: Lost Treasure on the Beach
A Passion for Plants: The Marie Selby Botanical Gardens
Pitching Paradise During the Roaring 20s

About the Author

Quintessential Sarasota: Stories and Pictures from the 1920s to the 1950s
Sarasota: A History
Sarasota: Roaring Through the 20s
Sarasota: A Sentimental Journey in Vintage Images
Sarasota: Then and Now
Spring Training in Sarasota, 1924–1960